Mother Mary Agnes, of the diocese of Aberdeen and Orkney, was born in Nottingham and spent her early years in a small mining village, the daughter of a fitter's mate and his handicapped wife. At an early age she was influenced by the life of Francis of Assisi, and also by the more spartan spirit of the Celtic Church. An introduction to Scotland added a touch of magic. All these, and the tragic early death of a much-loved mother, drew her inevitably towards the fulfilment of the religious life. After more than 20 years as a Sister in Devon she began a new religious life as a solitary on the remote island of Fetlar in Shetland. Here, she has been joined by other women seeking the same solitary life-style, and subsequently founded The Society of Our Lady of the Isles (SOLI).

**Jesus saith, Let not him who seeks cease
until he find, and when he finds he shall
be astonished . . .**

From the Oxyrynchus Papyri, third century

(*Our Bible in the Making*, Revd J. Paterson Smyth,
published by Sampson Low, Marston & Co.)

For Love Alone

Soli Deo

Mother Mary Agnes, SOLI

With illustrations by the author

First published in Great Britain in 2003 by
Society for Promoting Christian Knowledge
Holy Trinity Church
Marylebone Road
London NW1 4DU

British Library Cataloguing-in-Publication Data
A catalogue record for this book is available from the British Library

ISBN 0-281-05559-9

1 3 5 7 9 10 8 6 4 2

Typeset by WestKey Ltd, Falmouth, Cornwall
Printed in Great Britain by Bookmarque Ltd, Croydon, Surrey

Contents

Foreword

I still remember my first visit in 1992 as Bishop to the most northern part of the Diocese of Aberdeen and Orkney – the Shetland Islands. It was a cold and grey November, in the season of All Saints. Following a weekend of visits to the two congregations there, and meeting church and community leaders, I then travelled 50 miles north from the town of Lerwick to the small island of Fetlar. There I was to meet for the first time a religious sister, Sister Agnes, who had come eight years previously to live out a life of prayer on this extremely remote part of the British Isles. I wondered what I would find when I arrived at her home. Was she some kind of religious eccentric?

What I did receive on arrival at the Ness was a singularly warm welcome not only from Sister Agnes, but from Sister Mary Clare who had joined her in 1989, and Rosemary, a long-time companion and mentor of Sister Agnes. After the evening office we had a meal and delightful conversation filled with laughter. As I went to my room in one of the recently built visitor units, with a howling gale outside, I reflected on the paradox of that evening's experience – a life of prayer and contemplation, yet filled with laughter!

Over the years since then, I have visited Fetlar on many further occasions. There have been times of celebration – profession of Sisters, Sister Agnes becoming Mother Mary Agnes, the dedication of Lark's Hame, and the ordination of Mother as priest. There have also been times of struggle – the search to kindle and express the vision Sister Agnes came with; finding the right process of discernment for those wishing to share in the life of SOLI. At such times I saw another facet of this community: one that had to dig deep to discover, and sometimes re-discover, its roots in a life of prayer and contemplation.

The contrast of joy and laughter with the readiness to dig deep and discover at the heart of community a life built on prayer is what has attracted many people to take the long and at times hazardous route to the island of Fetlar. There they have found, even after a few days living as part of the SOLI community, how such an experience enriches and supports their daily lives when they return to Sheffield or Cornwall or Edinburgh or wherever. Living with SOLI is far from an 'escape'; it is an engagement with the God who will surprise us each day if we are open to him.

This is the fourth book written by Mother Mary Agnes, and it continues that story which began back in 1984. It is a story of her own personal journey, and of the community which she founded – the Society of Our Lady of the Isles (SOLI).

But this book is more than that. It is an invitation to all who read it to reflect on the presence and operation of God in their lives. For all of us need to keep re-discovering the God who is to be found in a life rooted in prayer; to be open to the God who surprises us each day; and to enjoy the God who shares in our laughter!

The Most Revd Bruce Cameron,
Bishop of Aberdeen and
Orkney, Primus

Prologue

With her nose, a small replica of her father's, glued against the window she gazed, fascinated, at the wonderland outside. It sparkled with a whiteness such as she had never known, and she wanted to wave her arms and mould her body and her whole being into the beauty of it, into this new phantasy world upon which her eyes were feasting. She had felt exactly the same when she watched her first piece of ballet on her family's television, for the dancing that flickered across the eight-inch screen had given her the feeling of soaring into another dimension. Later, she had tried some ballet of her own down the staircase, and found it easy, that it was all a matter of confidence and speed. Up she raced and down she skimmed, trying – and, amazingly, managing it – not to allow anything but the tips of her toes to touch the treads: that was, until her horrified mother discovered and stopped her. It was a freedom and a flying, and she longed to fly, to hurl herself into this strange, other region of beauty that beckoned and yet at the same time was oddly familiar. Indeed, these first stirrings of the spiritual had caused her to touch something that she already knew and yet could in no way have explained, or for that matter felt any need to explain – that is until now, fifty years later, as she sat at her desk and wrote. Yes, now, when she was certain that such feelings were stimulated by the insight that came with the innocence of childhood, an innocence that reached out and grasped at true wisdom; that lay hold of a long-lost gift, a purity, a knowledge; one which, in later life, age and so-called worldly understanding obscured. Was this yearning, which she had felt and amazingly still, in part, perceives, a reaching out for something that only our spirits were, in this life, able to discern? Was it a homing into an inbuilt, inner certainty that we were not just physical beings but that we were also souls?

The wintry weather of that long ago day had reshaped the garden in soft curves and fascinating forms. Snow was mounded into traceries on the latticework where the roses grew in the summer and over the gate that divided the front garden from the back. It was bowing the branches of the lilac and the fruit trees to the ground so that they looked like giant bears with extended arms. There were turreted castles, the habitation of princes, and mountain peaks, where fairies dwelt, and a deep forest under the currant bushes where a dragon lay waiting, listening, glistening, ready to pounce, ready to consume every flake of snowy splendour in a great billow of flame. She hoped that he would not, for she wanted the magic of this day to stay for ever that she might be drawn into its mysterious silence and solitude. She shivered a little, and then remembered the great King, he who was the Lord of all whiteness and wonder. No, nothing could ever harm her, least of all a dragon.

'Mam, can I go out?' she shouted in the direction of the kitchen.

'No, ma duck, its snowin too hard. Ya'll have ta wait until tomorra and we'll see what it's like then.'

'I could put ma slacks and ma wellies on . . . and ma big coat . . .'

'I want ta go anall,' Carole her sister cried out from upstairs where she was playing in her room.

'She's too little an she'll slip down, but I'd be alright, Mam. I'm good at slidin and I'll only take a minit ta walk arount gardan. I do want ta mek a slide. Can I . . . please?'

'No, ma duck, not today, it's too late. See, sun's goin down and it'll soon be dark.'

The sun of that long ago day sank as it was to sink a thousand days afterwards, allowing time itself to run its course in the spinning out of the years of that same child's life. Like a top it spun, spiralling her far from her Nottinghamshire village, and landing her instead at another new rising of the self-same orb, on a tiny island in the North Sea. And it was there that I (for the child was me) now sat on a low stool in the pointed gable window of Lark's Hame on Fetlar.

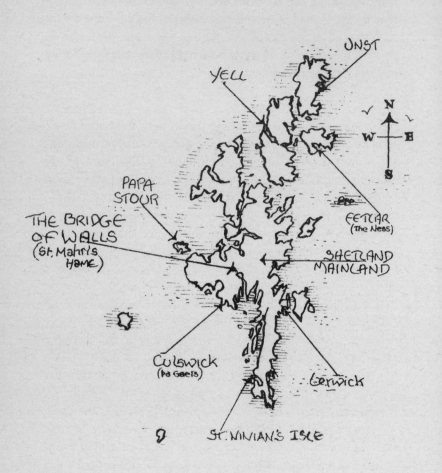

UNST

YELL

PAPA
STOUR

THE BRIDGE
OF WALLS
(St. Mahri's
Home)

FETLAR
(The Ness)

SHETLAND
MAINLAND

Culswick
(da Gaers)

Lerwick

St. NINIAN'S ISLE

N
W · E
S

1

Love's Call

It was almost dawn, and through the window the island would soon be unfolding into as glorious a picture as any of those long ago winter days of childhood, though at that point of the morning it was still framed by a dark sea. Listening to the roar of the wind, I waited for the first streaks of light to shoot across the water, and when they did I raised a hand to shade my eyes from the glare. We, in this small, northern, religious house of the Society of Our Lady of the Isles, lived out a hermit-type lifestyle and our first Office of the day was always said in this solitary fashion. Balancing the breviary on my lap, I flicked open the first page, though only to glance up again to find the room dimmed and cloud obscuring the view in another flurry of snow. Flakes swirled thickly into the glass, instantly congealing, then as quickly breaking and slithering down the panes in neat flotillas that piled into a blanket along the lower rim by my feet. Looking down, not wishing to encroach upon the sacredness of the hour by the lighting of a lamp, I sought to focus on the words in the open book. At that instant, heaven opened another eye, and in fascination I watched a second blink of sunlight widen into a shaft of gold. Again, brilliance pierced the storm, and sliding across the waters spilled pools of silken glory into the bay. Bending my head, I returned to the words of the dawn-hour Office of Prime.

V. In the beginning God created the heavens and the earth.
R. And God said, 'Let there be light' and there was light.[1]

Maybe there were moments of illumination in every life, when all the superfluous clutter, all the sometimes noisy, not so necessary, outer things, which the world called 'reality', dropped away, leaving behind only the starkness of what really was. It was as though everything slid into perspective and suddenly one was able, albeit fleetingly, to perceive truth, to see perfection – nakedly splendid – and how awesome that was. In the Hour of Prime, by the pointed window which reached down to the floor, this was one such moment when in a glimmer of the eternal, time seemed suddenly caught up in the spiralling dance of those glinting flakes, melting into the pane. The beauty outside held me, and for no more than an intake of breath, the reason for our existence became clear. Then, alas, as swiftly as it had come, the light spun away, faded, and was gone.

Shutting my eyes and allowing the few remaining swathes of night to creep back into the room, I repeated the opening words of Prime: 'In the beginning . . . the beginning . . .' How could one ever explain those dark depths of the beginning . . . ?

Night resettled its load, and I continued to ponder. Yes, 'In the beginning' there had been a formless void and darkness had covered the face of the deep . . . Yet out of those same depths had come life, and, we were told, we were brought forth.

Seconds flipped away and, how I did not know, a dark spiralling movement of energy swallowed me into itself, into that same beginning of all things, into an abyss. Down into a churning and swirling of waters, into a mounting rhythm, and then into a wild turbulent motion, where in a sea of sound and sense there came the knowledge of the voice . . . and the music and the voice spoke only one word – Love . . . Love . . . Love – over and over . . .

A grey furry head rubbed up against my knees and I felt two eyes staring pleadingly into mine. Glancing down, I smiled. 'I won't be long,' I murmured, and as if understanding, the creature turned, walked across the room and, pulling the door ajar with a paw, disappeared. Our other, more elderly, feline friend, Flugga, was still asleep on a chair. Good, I thought. At least Mooskit was not going to pester me to accompany him downstairs for food!

Turning back to my breviary to see if there was yet sufficient daylight to see the page, I noted with surprise that the veins in my hands were showing rather more prominently than I cared to acknowledge. Gosh, I thought, holding them closer, I'm growing old . . . A bit stunned, I found myself cogitating on a recent conversation with one of our more venerable friends. We had talked of the strangeness of seeing the human body suddenly showing signs of age, while inwardly folk remained immutable. Now, at 60, I understood. Welcome to the club, I breathed!

Of course, I appreciated that there was a great deal more to growing old than just the outer, physical deterioration of the body. Considering awhile, I decided that, probably, the whole concept of our existence in this world was much simpler than we realized, particularly since we were all such experts at missing the point. Could it be that within the aging process, the inner glory of our souls, like a butterfly, was simply undergoing a transformation, and that as it burgeoned into the fullness of the eternal, was assisting the outer chrysalis of our physical state to degenerate and fall away? Indeed, out of such a process one could begin to grasp that, even while here in this life, especially in our maturing years, we were provided with an incredible opportunity of abandoning ourselves into something literally out of this world! So, strange as it seemed, perhaps our hoarier years had the grand purpose of accelerating our journeying towards freedom! In which case, aging must be God's way of tumbling us forward towards the receiving of his amazing gift of the freedom of being, a gift which even during our mortal span could be touched and delighted in. If correct, then it would appear that with every increasing year we were tugged that bit nearer to the final curtain, when at the releasing of our soul in death, we would simply slide from one side to the other in the transition of our earthly selves into the heavenly. Consequently, I concluded that 'oldness' was merely the final mileage on the earthly stage of an eternal journey.

The door eased shut after Moosy, whose feline frame was also beginning to show signs of age. This I minded, for we were far from ready to say goodbye to him. However, unlike us, cats wasted little time with such concerns. Indeed, the levy of the years could, for us humans, be decidedly grim, for how could anyone think that decrepitude indicated a loving God's little-by-little way of releasing the soul? Yet, in life's contrary manner, how consoling this unbinding procedure, this pilgrimage towards Love really was to those who believed. Albeit, in the end, whatever any of us felt or believed, there was no denying that we were all fellow travellers on a journey, in which the entire spectrum of days, nights, weeks, years, and each rising and setting of the sun, patiently unravelled a whole pageant of life. Thus, in our travelling through this earthly time, we were spiralled, if we lived long enough, through all the hoped-for joys of youth, the likely middle-aged sorrows, and – who knew? – perhaps now in my case, into the glorious experience of growing old.

Staring through the snowy patterns on the window, I realized afresh how we each lived out a totally different drama of life in a given era. And yet, it was always within that same cycle, a cycle which spun us along whatever route we allowed it to carry us, which hopefully was one of God's choosing. Taking into account his gift of free will to humankind, which of us could ever be certain what the future might bring? My mind ran on, telling me that 'time', then, was a sort of earthly vehicle which ultimately transported us all, if we would, towards the wholeness of love. That it should take its toll physically was a mere detail, and one, I supposed, which had to be accepted as a necessary part of an otherwise exciting process. Age-wise, there was nothing much we could do about it, anyway, except to go with the flow – a flow which, God willing, would convey us, wrinkles and all, into that same Love's perfection.

A more sustained light fell across my breviary, and I knew that I must concentrate on saying Prime. Of course, 'Love' was the subject of my next book, a subject, which was paramount to everything else in my life, a subject that was for me, what life and eternity were all about.

I looked down.

'In the beginning . . .'

Tiresomely, my mind and memory wandered again, this time through the years to SOLI's beginnings, to the onset of our own spiritual journey as a family in God.

Forty years earlier, at 19, and much to everyone's surprise, most of all my own, I had entered an Anglican Franciscan convent in Devon, There, for 21 years I had lived and learned the lessons of a disciplined yet simple religious lifestyle. Towards the end of that time I had received a call within a call, which necessitated my moving away from the community and along a new road – a road which, rather amazingly, I was given permission to pursue. The call had been towards a deepening of vocation, and one which brought me to Scotland. Most procedures of detachment were painful and, humanly speaking, this particular severing was especially so, albeit that it was with the Bishop of Exeter's blessing and with my vows held intact. Yet my heart, in that contradictory way which hearts have, and despite any difficulties, sang for joy at the privilege of being allowed to test this new way of life.

In due course, finding myself on Fetlar, a remote Shetland isle, I lived out God's directive – a simple, joyful lifestyle, based on the Gospels. My hopes were of sharing the vocation with a family of others, whom in my naivety I expected God to send at once to join me. I was mistaken, and with surprise found myself living as a solitary for four and a half years. It was during this time that the first real yearnings for a hermit lifestyle became apparent. Actually, this unexpected discovery of solitude swung me violently into hoping that I had got the whole 'vision' thing wrong and that God, all along, meant me to stay on my own and develop the hermit vocation. Certainly, as SOLI looked back, it was clearer to perceive that, both as individuals and as a group, we, like all God's children, only saw 'through a glass darkly', and that mostly it was in the participation of his step-by-step process that he revealed the way forward. Perhaps this tantalizingly slow, experience-by-experience pilgrimage of learning only what we needed to know at a given time was our Creator's best way of moulding each of us into his plan for the future. Amazingly, as I now traced back through the years, I could see how all that SOLI had experienced during those early years of growth was necessary, and how all things, however strange they may have seemed at the time, did ultimately 'work together for good' when we truly loved God.

So, very positively, I now saw that those solitary years, although not exactly planned, had been meant, for in them I had been given time to question the future, and in the experience and vulnerability of that period to reach a signpost pointing in three different directions.

The first arm pointed along a road which said: 'To the Mixed Life', which was the type of religious lifestyle I had once lived with the Franciscans in Devon, and which to start with confused me into assuming that God meant us to continue living as Franciscans on Fetlar. Doubtless, I inclined in that direction because the first people who joined me were so much more given to this form of spirituality, which was a mix of both the active and contemplative states. Indeed, that was how we, as the first SOLI group, had started off, though I have to say that I felt thoroughly uncomfortable with the route and learned only through unfolding years that it was not the right way.

The second arm of the signpost pointed along another pathway, this one marked: 'To a Group of Hermits', and strangely this option of living a contemplative life in separate hermitages yet coming together for worship sat much more comfortably with me. As a matter of fact, I found it difficult to apprehend why my earlier companions were so adamantly against the idea, and in the end reluctantly accepted that the mixed life should be tried. However, and, you may understand, despite our going forward along this route, there was still much compromise on my part. Ultimately, this showed itself in our eventual defining of the more solitary leaning of the Sisters from that of the mixed way of the Associates. Thus, in separating the role of the Sisters, we began to form the surrounding circle of those whom we now called 'Companions'. Therefore, as SOLI stood, Companions were those who had a 'mixed life' calling. This meant that although they had committed themselves to being an integral, supporting part of our contemplative religious family, they also had the freedom to reach out to others. In contrast, the Sisters did not participate in outside socializing, excepting with permission, though they had their own outreach. It was simply that a Sister's ministry was a different, more hidden vocation, exercised from her hermitage. By reason of these differences it had now been decided that any aspirant to SOLI began her journey of discernment in the capacity of a 'Seeker'. This period of one year we found to be a necessary requirement, in order to determine more solidly her true calling.

The last option on my signpost towards SOLI's future was hardly an option at all for the third arm pointed to 'The [solitary] Hermit Life'. This possible developing of the single hermit lifestyle was what I was most drawn towards. Yet such a way would have meant the laying aside of any vision of that 'spiritual family' which I was certain God had asked me to form.

Now, almost two decades later and after sundry twists and turns, SOLI had found its answer. Our vocation was quite simply the call of love, a call which at its root was the same summons, which came to everyone and was the sole purpose for living. To fulfil this command, in whatever way we were asked, was all we asked, and certainly its fruits manifested themselves in a million ways. So, for SOLI, its spirituality was finally grasped in our living as a group of hermits.

In working towards our consolidation as a religious community, the true contemplative nature of SOLI's spirituality emerged. Excitingly, a strong Celtic flavour of lifestyle had already grown out of our Franciscan roots, and later in its blossoming began to bear fruit that had a hint of Carthusianism about it. What a mixture, you might think, although you will also comprehend that there was a natural process within which all aspects of SOLI's growth ripened into something that was neither purely Franciscan, Celtic nor Carthusian, but rather a recipe that blended all three – and more, resulted in something that was uniquely itself. When folk ask us now what and who we are, we invariably reply: we are SOLI!

Hence, God had brought forth SOLI, the Society of Our Lady of the Isles, and in the solitude of dawn and in the ebbing and flowing of my own prayer, while the visibility of the moment came and went, my thoughts widened to embrace this little group of those whom I now thought of as family. Those dear friends who over the past twenty years had ventured to join me here, to become witnesses of the great King whom I had loved as a child. They were women who, at the end of my period of living alone in The Ness, the tiny croft house on the tip of our windblown peninsula, felt called by God, as I did, to come to this isle. There was no doubt in my mind that each of them had been sent – they who were so different and so unique.

Rosemary, the first to arrive, was a stalwart and much loved companion. Sadly, after fifteen years she died of lung cancer. Next came Mary, a widow, who was the first to join me in the sense of becoming a Sister. Given the name of Sister Mary Clare, she stayed with us on Fetlar for ten years, though was now seconded to help with a project in Orkney. Soon after Mary's arrival, Rose, a nurse, landed here, stayed a year or so and then decided to continue her vocation in nursing, eventually moving south for a time. Overlapping with Rose came Frances, a church musician, who also stayed for a time until she too returned to England. Jacqueline, later to become Sister Mary Aidan, joined us next, and now, a decade later and my deputy, she is currently based at St Mahri's Hame, on the Shetland Mainland. Along with Jacqueline, Pat arrived from New Zealand, although after a few months of postulancy she also left us to re-embrace a teaching career. Then had come Sybil, whom I had first met when, as a visitor, she came to Fetlar during my early days on the island, and who, having sold her house in Reading, was now, along with Jean from America, a SOLI Companion. Only a short time after Jean had settled, a young woman by the name of Alison also joined us, subsequently becoming Sister Mary Cuthbert; since I had moved into Lark's Hame, the house on the cliff, she now 'bides', as they say in these parts, at The Ness, the original croft house which was once my home. There, she grows most of our vegetables. I have a dream that, one day, other Sisters might have a tiny patch of ground attached to their hermitage, where they too could share the joys of gardening. So, although three of those early supporters were called to continue their spiritual pilgrimages elsewhere (for Rose, now returned to us, was living in Rosemary's old croft house) those of us who stayed in Shetland had continued to be moulded by God into SOLI – which, as you will see, consisted of four Sisters, two Companions and one Seeker.

So it was that God wove intricate patterns of flight in his flocks which were wonderful to behold, especially (speaking in the literal sense) since none of his feathered creatures ever seem one too many or out of place as they wheel in formation, following their own path of flight.

The snow still fell heavily, though such thoughts of flight brought blinks of our Shetland summer to mind, of terns screaming over the lochs and gulls circling the Ness Point and dipping into the sea. However, a sudden sneaky draught whistling between the window frame and its casing brought me back to the reality of the season with a bump. Rising, I stepped across the room to turn up a heater. Never mind, I decided, returning to my stool, be it winter or summer, there was always joy and that wonderful sense of freedom . . . for without doubt Shetland was the kind of locality where we, SOLI, could delight in our part in God's pageant and passage through time.

In a room now rose-coloured I concentrated anew on the saying of the Divine Office. With eyes closed, I re-entered that place where the ticking of life's clock merged with heaven; where the Church, the King's family, the beloved children of God, all those who like us had chosen love, who had chosen life over death, had become one, in the great volume of worship and praise which ascended unceasingly to him from a million lips in every part of the world.

Now that the daylight fills the sky,
We lift our hearts to God on high . . .[2]

'We lift our hearts . . .' Yes, I thought, 'we lift our hearts', we let go and risked taking flight, as the child had taken flight down the stairs. We abandoned ourselves to our dearest God, who stooped in Christ to catch us into the dance, and revolved us ever closer to himself. Snowflakes spiralled with fresh vigour against the pane as thoughts of the past, and particularly of those early members of SOLI and of SOLI's own deepening contemplative vocation, floated in and out of my mind like the coming and going of the sunlight. Supposedly, the relevant thing was not so much the way in which we let go and flew, but the knowledge that in whatever ungainly manner we released our hold on the things of this world there was a real need to do so. There was a need to trust and to let go, in order to be lifted up and live.

Reaching out to tap snow from the window I saw that the sea had misted over once more. In the beginning of time the Holy Spirit had moved across the face of the waters . . . Here, over the waters, over the huddle of dwellings of Aithness, all was transformed once more into whiteness. The sun would be scattering its beams elsewhere, but here all was hushed whiteness and waiting. Silently, I too held my breath, hoping, as always, to discern the next turnings of the way forward into the future, hoping to be led clearly into the next new chapters of life. And, as said, it was not only a waiting on my own, but now it was a joyful waiting with others of the same heart and mind, despite the departure of some of my earlier companions. It was a waiting in solitude and in prayer with SOLI, the order of women whom God had established for his own particular purpose on this tiny isle.

Remarkably, this place, our home, our hermitages on the Aithness peninsula of Fetlar, had become, as its name 'Aithness' suggested, 'the point between', and for me it would always be the point between heaven and earth. Now, as I gazed at the outer world, all moments merged physically, in the obscurity of the snow, and spiritually, in the becoming one in a dimension where there were no limits or boundaries and where each of us was detached enough from self to be growing, however slowly, into who God meant us to be. Here, in Shetland, SOLI embraced a type of lifestyle which, to the minds of many, 'imprisoned'. At least, that is how most of the world seemed to see it, yet in this place we had all begun to learn, albeit falteringly, the first real lessons of freedom, the freedom of the birds. We had begun to grasp the kind of simplicity that sets souls at liberty to be who they are and eventually to soar above the blizzard of the unseeing to a place of perceiving, or at least to the place of glimpsing, however briefly, that which lies beyond. Undoubtedly, our life here on this remote isle was simple, perhaps too simple for many to embrace; nevertheless, those of us whom God had called rejoiced in it, and whatever anyone thought, here at last SOLI had found the 'point between'.

Prime over but for a final prayer of praise, my heart lifted to him who held all things in his sway. Glad to be alone, that is apart from Flugga, I watched the remains of another shaft of light lick the waters. The swell heaved and fell, rolling forward into the bay or the 'wick' as it is known up here in these far northerly isles. Yet as I continued to watch, abruptly the light faded, swallowing the sea again into oblivion, a breeze arose and a new blizzard took hold, gathering itself for further fray. Then, whirling into extraordinary spectral shapes, it spread outwards, fanning further and further, folding and unfolding itself into angels' wings. Ghostly wisps of cloud stretched thinly and then more thickly and then thinly again to the far corners of the earth, and I, who so long ago had longed to fly, framed the last words of the Office by heart:

Thanks be to you, O God, that we have risen, today,
to the rising of life itself.[3]

The Joys of Love

2

Love Conceived

As the door flung open its thud shattered the silence, causing me to whip round from where I stood by the sink in my galley kitchen in the roof of Lark's Hame. Mooskit strode towards me, his feline body taut, his tail upright, waving like a banner. Seeing me looking down at him he paused, stared back, relaxed a little and sidled around the hem of my woollen habit. Then, bending his head, he butted my legs, at first cajolingly, though increasingly persistent, for he knew that I was no easy prey. He also knew that the cat food was downstairs.

'Moosy, couldn't you go down and find Sybil?' I suggested. 'You know that she always gives you breakfast.' Wiping my hands I pulled out the breadboard and spread a couple of rice cakes with honey.

He rammed me again. 'She's not there . . . She should be . . . You come . . .' Pausing for a moment, his nose in the air, he regarded me intently, eyes blazing. He waited, then blinked, frowned and suddenly, consumed with feline haughtiness, jumped on to the chair by the skylight. There, silently, with the straightest of backs and feigning a nonchalance that I knew he did not feel, he stared at the frozen window. 'Ugh, cold, and nobody cares about cats!' He wiggled one self-conscious ear, his demeanour oozing displeasure and his now flashing tail speaking volumes.

Reaching towards him, I stroked a hand down his sleek coat. A ripple of movement ran down his spine, but immediately he stiffened, continuing to stare at the glass. 'It'll be all right, boy, truly it will. You're a good puss, but you need to be patient.'

Mooskit, whose Shetland name meant 'mouse-coloured-grey', was a large grey cat with white markings on his paws and face and under his chin. Inappropriately – at least we thought it inappropriate – the beautiful white fur beneath his chin ran down his chest in the shape of preaching bands! Stiffly he continued to peruse the white pane, not at all convinced by my patter.

'It'll be all right' or 'all will be well' are often words we use as a form of comfort or consolation, and how lightly we use them. Switching off the kettle I poured the steaming water into a mug and stirred my coffee. Someone else had used them too, I mused,

Mooskit

though in a much deeper and more significant way. Yes, Dame Julian, that anchorite of long ago, had used them and she was absolutely right, of course: all was well, whatever I, or even Mooskit, might be churning around in our tiny minds, or whatever ups and downs any of us might have. Indeed, despite the fragility of our existence, human or animal, set on a planet within a universe that we know so little about, God has assured us that not only were all things well but that 'all manner of things' would continue to 'be well'. Certainly, I knew that this was true, at least for those who loved, because for them all things were rooted and grounded in him who was Love, and, as I had not so very long ago recited in the dawn-hour Office, 'without him was not anything made, that was made'.

Yes, I pondered, within God was all comfort and assurance, the assurance that he had come among us and experienced our life in this world; that he had been born, like us, in the flesh, and of a woman, and had been open to the fleeting joys of mankind, to the same elements of pride as we, open to the world's darkest suffering, and also to the glory of knowing that all things could be conquered by Love.

So, for me, Christ's life was the most unique of all stories of love, for upon it, with all its mysterious threads of joy, sorrow and glory, was based every other, as was every chapter of this book in its sharing with you the story of our own lives within SOLI.

In spite of the snow still covering the skylight the room was cheery. Lifting Mooskit from the chair I sat and sipped my coffee. The red glow of the fire warmed my heart, and full of gratitude I began to trace the pattern of Our Lord's incarnation on earth.

Had the life of Christ's mother been as simple as mine, I wondered? Had she loved with the intensity with which a creature can love? And had she, Mary, been in her home, a home she had cared about as I cared about mine, when the angel had visited her, when the Holy Spirit had come upon her? Had her life, at least in part, been as happily ordinary? Slipping both hands around my mug, I continued to speculate. Had she been called by God, as we of SOLI had all been called, to a certain life-style? Ours, of course, was comparatively simple, but hers . . . Was hers rather more dramatically spectacular, something like the weather outside? Whichever way, and more likely than not it was a mixture of both, I knew that it would have been a million times more meaningful.

Mooskit pricked up both his ears, and I listened too and heard the same sounds from below. In a flash he scuttled off my knee and from the room. Sybil was opening a tin! Having shut the door after him, I raised the mug to my mouth again, for I liked my coffee hot, and reseating myself I returned to my reflections on SOLI's beloved patron.

In a more mysterious way than any other human, Mary had been caught up by that force, that energy and mighty power of the Great High King himself, and her whole being had quickened into the wholeness and holiness of life. It must have been a kind of new awakening, a falling in love. Yet what of all those ordinary, minor details of the story? Was she, this uncomplicated girl who was called to be Christ's mother, alone at the time? We could be fairly certain that she was, for whether there were others nearby or not and there probably were, everything would have been blocked out by her oneness in him, her extraordinary one-to-one communion, her colloquy with God, with Love himself, out of whom was to be born the Word of Life. In her there would have been the purity that comes from simplicity rather than from any enforced holiness. I would expect that she was a 'normal' girl, with no clutter of pious baggage or rigorous religious training. And whether this incredible occurrence, this moment of the world's most profound intimacy, took place in a room or out of doors, or whether it was in the morning or evening, in the cold or in the warmth, or whether she was sitting, standing or kneeling is of little importance. Instead, all that did matter was what we had been told – that she, chosen in her simplicity, was overwhelmingly moved by the angel's words and incredulous of what was to be! The King, 'the Holy Spirit, the Spirit of Love, had come upon her' and it was certain that he came to her as never before to any other human creature. Oh to be so free as to say, with her, 'Be it unto me according to thy word,' and oh, the wonder of how God's profundity speaks through the artless clarity of such souls.

The whiteout continued throughout that day, and outside and beyond every snow-shuttered window came whispers of wind. Later the wind rose with more wind behind it, churning the sea into storm, and Shetland was brought to a halt. All that was loose was re-battened or lost to the cliffs. Folk clung to their hearths, banging shut their doors, and apart from the scurrying out, at intervals, to check and feed their sheep around the drifts, no one stirred. Only the snow-plough moved back and forth across the single-track road, keeping the way open for the island nurse. We, like our neighbours, checked our food stores, our gas lamps and candle stock in case of power cuts. Oil was double-checked too and fuel lugged in for the fire. More gales were forecast, planes were grounded, and what few ships had been out on the ocean were brought in and anchored – brought in, that was, on the Shetland Mainland and other Shetland isles, though not on Fetlar. Fetlar had no harbour, only a docking berth for the ro-ro ferry. Elsewhere, the island's three or four rowing boats had been tied up long before the grips of winter began.

I wondered how Sister Mary Clare was faring in her now more active life in Orkney, and how Sister Mary Aidan, two ferry journeys away from Fetlar on the Shetland Mainland at Browland, was managing to keep warm and survive the weather conditions. I had driven Sister Mary Aidan home after Christmas, knowing that a pipe in the roof of St Mahri's Hame had sprung a leak, though what we did not know at the time was exactly how much devastation it had caused. People sometimes imagined that in our idyllic life here nothing much ever went wrong, but since we lived in the same unpredictable world as everyone else, we were open to the same ups and downs, some of which, I am sure, Our Lady must also have experienced in Nazareth. It was precisely such hardships, of course, which provided us with the opportunity of spiritual growth. Without adversity, we might all have been a little insipid.

On the occasion of the Mahri's Hame disaster we had arrived in a car loaded with extra buckets, mops, Sister's luggage and, of course, Barney and Pippin the Browland cats, who always accompanied her to Fetlar. With exclamations of horror as we walked in through the door, we found Sister Mary Aidan's neighbours ankle-deep in water, pulling up carpets and piling furniture on top of furniture. It would take months of work to restore this now icebox of a home to rights, a place where suddenly there was no heating and everything was damp. Semi-camping there with Sister, I stayed for a week until we had achieved at least some semblance of order, though I must say it was a time not entirely devoid of frayed nerves! Thankfully, the insurance covered the repairs to the ceiling, the replacement of a piece of furniture and a new carpet. Now, with several weeks of work completed and normal life more possible, Sister could, at last, embark on the answering of SOLI's Christmas mail, a massive job she undertook for the community.

As I guessed, those weeks of the blizzard were wild ones and I thanked God that, over at Browland, Sister Mary Aidan was now warm. Nevertheless, despite such vicissitudes I always loved this time of year, especially when we were snowbound, for in a way it perfectly described the hidden nature of our life. Actually, for me, the concealment caused by snow always brought deep feelings of an at-oneness with life, and cosiness with God. Likewise, thoughts of a ship's anchor plunging to the depths of the ocean caused me to pause and consider our vocation, the parallel being that an anchor, once dropped, could not be seen, and yet it was this which held the tossing vessel safely on the surface. In the same way it was, I supposed, that hermits and solitaries were called to be anchors, for, dropped into the deeps and unseen, they helped hold the surface things fast. And, perhaps, who knew, it was precisely such people who held the spiritual life fast on the seas of a tempestuous world. Whatever, to my mind some souls were specifically called to this type of life. Mary and Joseph and Christ himself spent most of their lives hidden. Similarly, SOLI's life became more and more a life of seclusion, and out of it, as with the holy family, love burgeoned. 'Why bury yourselves in this kind of way?' folk sometimes asked, and yet, as the scriptures said, 'unless a grain of wheat falls into the earth and dies, it remains just a single grain; but if it dies, it bears much fruit'.[1] Likewise, unless an anchor was dropped into the depths it could not hold the ship secure. Truly, in SOLI's hidden life there was a purpose, and its purpose was – LOVE . . . And yes, I thought, in Christ's mother that same seed of love was sown in human form, and began to grow in the hermitage of her womb. Buried deep within her heart she would have known and treasured, as Mother Julian was later to know and write and as we in SOLI know, that love was the meaning.

As the moon and the sun took their course and the tides ebbed and flowed, so the rhythm of the days passed, and as another new morning dawned, back in the same kitchen at the same time of day I reached for an apple from the fruit bowl, and sliced it in half. Beyond words, I knew that love was our vocation and that the seed of love was growing in that hidden, spiritual womb of SOLI.

The snow was still drifting, and popping a piece of apple into my mouth I wondered if supplies might get short, and whether our stocks would hold out. They usually did, for we were used to being stormbound. A moment or two later, washing up my plate and mug I put them away and made my way to the gallery, overlooking the chapel. The Chapel of Christ the Encompasser and all his Holy Angels was unoccupied at that hour, yet the stalls below seemed strangely full. Maybe that small building was filled with a host of immortal ones . . . yes, with who knew or could guess how many angels or saints? Rosemary was probably close, and all those others whom we loved and who, though briefly passed from sight, were still loving us.

Perching on the edge of a seat I looked down at the altar, spread with white cloths for Mass, and my heart rejoiced that Christ was so central to our life. His presence was always incredibly tangible in this holy place, this 'point between', where the veil was so thin. Truly, it was a place of drawing nearer to God – not only for us, but for our guests too, especially at worship. It was interesting, I thought, that those who visited were almost always folk who, in a mysterious way, had been propelled here. They were people who, it would appear, had been called in this direction for some purpose – not least to step aside to plumb the depths. So, already for many, SOLI had become a place of rediscovering God, or themselves. A place of challenge, of finding a new ministry or a deepening of vocation, it was also a point of healing and an oasis of peace. And hopefully, for all, it would continue to be a place of seeking, finding and of grace.

Folk visited from far and near, and stayed for anything from a few days to a fortnight between May and September, months when the daylight hours were longer. Outside these months the weather was often inclement, added to which there was a great need for the community, Sisters and Companions alike, to find time to take stock – to tank up physically, mentally and spiritually. Therefore, those more inhospitable, wilder, winter months were, in fact, essential to us, and explained why visitors were welcomed at Aithness during the summer months only. During that time, private self-catering accommodation, with all facilities, could be booked. That the visitors saw little of the Sisters in a social manner in no way detracted from their being able to touch the love of God profoundly. Indeed, I knew that this was often all the more paramount by reason that the lifestyle was a hidden one.

A door below opened and shut. That would be Sybil. She was speaking to someone, who sounded like a grey cat wanting to go out via the front entrance! After a moment or two a second door clicked and silence was restored. In a couple of hours SOLI would be assembling for Mattins and the Eucharist, and then there would be a choir practice. Afterwards, Sister Mary Cuthbert had arranged to see me, to discuss the replacing of the barn roof. Later, Jean wanted to talk about a music project, and after that, during the afternoon, Rose was coming to help with a pile of photocopying, and to show me her newly designed booklet of visitor information.

'It's wonderful, isn't it,' I said to Rose later, over a cup of tea, 'how visitors are increasingly being touched by Our Lord's presence here, and are actually stating, themselves, how imperative it is that SOLI's quietness be preserved.' In point of fact, without realizing it, guests now added their own dimension to the life, so helping strengthen our resolve to safeguard that which we counted so precious. Certainly, Aithness, this 'point between', needed to be protected from unnecessary clamour. However, this did not mean that visitors had to tiptoe around or keep a rigid silence with each other. It was simply that SOLI was grateful to them for respecting its quietness. Having said that, visitors were not totally isolated, for if they wished, time and opportunity could always be made to meet members of the community and talk.

Our gratitude knew no bounds for the encouragement we had received from many people, though inevitably, like most

Christian groups, we could not expect the whole world to understand what we were about. As would be expected, it appeared to some that this small Episcopalian religious community sat in the far north 'doing nothing'. Howbeit, we certainly strove to follow a truly authentic call and, rather surprisingly, out of our obedience SOLI seemed to have become a focal point, a kind of lighthouse, a 'soul centre' and a place of 'being' to many. Most people realized, of course, that before they could do anything for God, they first of all had to discover who they 'were', since one's 'doing' came out of one's 'being'. What SOLI did, because it constantly touched its own identity in Christ (whether shovelling snow, washing the dishes, providing hospitality, worshipping in chapel or anything else) was to create a temple of God, a place for his use, a place to which at least a few souls could step aside to touch Christ at a deeper level. Others, of course, were united with us through a deep bond of prayer. Consequently, we were not in the business of providing a hotel for the Church or some sort of Christian holiday centre. Instead, we provided a God-centre of worship and prayer, and only after that offered accommodation, a place where people could stay alongside a monastic, contemplative lifestyle; where they could touch a lifestyle immersed in God . . . a lifestyle that was fully human, cherishing, Celtic in flavour and totally centred in love.

Bending my head and in union with all those others, I lifted my heart to Love himself.

3

Love Carried

With winter rapidly receding the days took their course, and one morning, sitting at my desk, in the room I called my office, I stared out at the view. Entranced by the sun casting sharp shadows into the hollows of the hill beyond The Ness, I ruminated on the next chapter of my new book, and not least on the ways in which we also, as humans, reflected light and cast shadows. It was still too cold to open the window, yet the day had a feeling of springtime about it. Almost overnight, the grass had become a haze of green, the snow had vanished, the bleached

Shuna in the snow by the bell

look of winter had disappeared and there were gaggles of oyster-catchers striding over the cliff around our buildings. Watching Sister Mary Cuthbert meander up the narrow road behind the croft house, I saw her pause every so often to allow Kelpie, the elderly cairn whom she had taken on after Rosemary's death, to stop to explore new scents along the track. Our other SOLI dog, Shuna, in a slightly long-suffering manner, lived here in Lark's Hame along with Flugga and Mooskit, and spent most of her time between Sybil's home, downstairs, and my hermitage space in the roof.

At that juncture, with Sybil away south, all three animals were draped around my feet. Switching off the computer, I stood up. Instantly alert, Shuna's ebullience knew no bounds. This was exactly the signal for which she had been waiting, and leaping into action, she voiced her elation; at last, her own walk was imminent. 'Stop!' I demanded, though knew, with the best will in the world, it was an impossible request. Sidestepping the dog's excited barking and gymnastic display, I crossed the room, only to zigzag back, and drop into my chair. 'No! Sit and stay, Shuna!' I said. She hesitated, then, reluctantly obedient, lowered her rear to the floor and placed her chin on my lap. 'Oh Shuna, lovey, I'm so sorry, Sister Mary Aidan's expecting me to ring her.'

I dialled the number. 'Hello Sister, it's me.'

'Oh hello, Mother, I was just about to ring you re the news-letter. I've almost finished typing it and I want your approval. Can I read it out?'

Pushing vigorously against my thigh, Shuna whined and, unflagging to the end, pawing my knee, reminded me of a friend's comment that if dogs did not have such long noses they would be able to speak! Avoiding the now riveting gaze, I looked away. Shuna whined again, licking my hand. 'Sorry, girl . . . Sorry, Shu . . . No, no . . . Stop . . . Can you just hang on a moment or two longer?'

Among other things, Sister Mary Aidan looked after the bulk of SOLI's communications, whether by telephone, e-mail or letter-writing. Over the years these tasks had multiplied, becoming even more of a mission for her than they had once been for me. This being so, Sister's neighbour, our Caim Member, Wilma, voluntarily and generously assisted her on several fronts, though primarily as office staff. One of the main reasons for her living in what I always thought of as our 'priory house', on the Shetland Mainland roughly fifty miles from SOLI's home base on Fetlar, was that it was important to have a Sister there, someone who could fulfil certain public relations duties. Obviously, such a person needed to be sufficiently mature to maintain the spiritual rhythm of our vocation on her own, yet also to be a solitary at heart. Being eremitical yet having equal ability to communicate with people on several levels was, undoubtedly, an unusual mix, though one which Sister Mary Aidan possessed. She, of all the community, was able to stand at the periphery, at the gate as a kind of Portress Sister. Added to which, experience had taught us that it was often easier to act as an intermediary between a contemplative community and the world at large from such a gatehouse position. It was also clear that from this geographically more accessible location, one was better able to see the distant perspective, and therefore more able to guide the movements of those who came and went. Consequently, people thinking they might make a journey to our island of Fetlar, or alternatively go off in an outward direction elsewhere, often visited Sister Mary Aidan first.

Shuna dropped to the floor and, showing only the whites of her eyes, gave me a mournful glance!

The fact that Sister Mary Aidan took care of our correspondence in no way inferred that other SOLI members were strictly unavailable. Officially, Sister Mary Cuthbert was on the telephone at certain times of the day for business calls, Rose for visitor information and bookings, and I, constantly informed of all that came in and went out, was on hand when necessary.

As well as being our prime communicator, Sister Mary Aidan was also SOLI's Novice Guardian, and this second office meant that not only did she need to be grounded theologically and in the rudiments of the religious life, but also to be a person who could set an example of how the life was to be lived. All Seekers, Aspirants and Novices spent some time with her at St Mahri's Hame, and we found that this arrangement worked well. So, in short, Sister Mary Aidan looked after the training for Novices and saw to most of SOLI's mail, which meant keeping in touch, particularly with the Caim.

The 'Caim', a Celtic word meaning encompassment or the circle around, was the name which Rosemary and I had come up with in the early days of our being on Fetlar. After months of racking our brains for a suitable word to describe those who had become associated with us in a looser-knit way than either the Sisters or the Companions, the title Caim proved exactly right. Interestingly, over the past few years we had noted with pleasure that other groups had also begun to use it. Anyway, it long ago became the name for the circle of friends whom we thought of as our extended spiritual family, a body of almost a hundred associates scattered throughout Britain and abroad.

Like Sister Mary Aidan, each of the Sisters and Companions took their share of the necessary activities of the common-life, for whoever one was or whatever one's gifts, we all had to live, and therefore to work. In other words, the telephone needed to be answered, letters written, the cooking and the shopping done, accounts kept, and the garden and buildings maintained and cleaned, an endless list . . . Of course, many of those jobs required certain outside interaction with people, and from such employment no one was exempt. This being so, we protected the solitary aspect of the vocation by a spreading of the workload. Had the lifestyle not been arranged in this way, it would quickly have been thrown out of kilter. So, all in all, our call was protected, and we continued to learn from experience that it was far easier for the Sisters to live hermitically, within a monastery set-up, than more vulnerably outside it. Alone, one was open to the culture and noise of a modern society, open to a life where there were few spiritual safeguards and little protection from a battering world. Here, at SOLI, however solitary our leanings, we understood the saying that no man was an island, and that within a balanced framework such as ours it was essential for us all to share willingly in what was required. Work-wise, I certainly had needed to learn how to delegate.

Half an hour later, clicking Shuna's lead on to her collar, we set off up the same road along which Sister Mary Cuthbert had walked earlier. The dog pranced forward though soon settled to a steady pace. Of course, I considered, my mind still flitting around the telephone call with Sister, Our Lady had also known about relating to people. She had needed to communicate with her cousin Elizabeth, to share a secret . . . to tell her of that incredible mystery . . . As so often when I walked, my thoughts turned to her. And yes, Mary, too, had walked, perhaps even skipped or sang, over the hills as she carried the Lord of Light, as she carried the Divine Communicator himself in her womb, and bore the enormous significance of his Word in her heart.

As I suspected, it was much colder outside than it looked, and as always on these occasions I was especially grateful to be wearing a habit. Our tweed winter tunic was oatmeal in colour, came down to our feet and was simply a robe, cut in the shape of a cross. We tied a knotted cord around our waist, and wore a cowled scapular over the habit when in chapel. The whole garb was simple, comfortable and – not least – 'covered a multitude of sins', as they say! Even so, the best thing about it was that one had little need to think of what to put on in the mornings!

The sunshine was now dazzling and I found that a few more migratory birds had returned to our shores. The sheep too were basking in the sudden waft of spring. This first season, as far north as Shetland, was short, in fact barely more than a whisper that summer was around the corner. On such a day it was a happy occupation to walk Shuna, if only up the right of way, and certainly an opportunity to think and pray.

Accelerating into another gear, my mind ran on around the book, with all that I wanted to say, and more importantly grasping its essence. It was to be summed up in the title long ago planned – *SOLI DEO*, or in other words *For God Alone* – though on account of its tenor I was tempted to call the volume *For Love Alone*. Love was my subject, so whatever I wrote would relate to love, to all that love was and should be in our lives. Every chapter would be about love, and whatever the result, the work itself would be for 'Love, alone'. Yes, ridiculous though it was, I wanted to write a book about the impossible. I wanted to capture love, and put it into words. I wanted to write about that incredible force, which created the universe and beyond, and which continued to evolve our world into the will of God. I wanted to write about that which evolved love into Love, and we humans into perfection . . . So, the story would be about the life-giving, energizing purport of love, about love flowing through the mysteries of the life of Christ and through the so often mysterious lives of his children. It would be about love as reflected in human beings, through their bodies, minds and spirits, and about a family of people called to risk everything in their standing unprotected before Love for Love's own sake. More, it would tell of their growth towards that longed-for and eternal union with Love himself. Yes, the work would be about SOLI: not a handbook of our calling, for that was contained in the Rule, but about the substance of the life and its purpose; a simple book relating to simple people, and written to share with any other simple souls who wished to read it. Yet, however simple an explanation of our life one managed to produce, again, in that same contradictory way that Christianity has, I wanted it to be a drawing out of the impossible from the depths of SOLI's vocation!

St John of the Cross, John Donne and others in the past had tried to say the impossible and, in part, for no one could do more than 'in part', had given the world inspiration. Of course, poets, artists and musicians had endeavoured throughout the centuries to catch the profound simplicity of 'truth', as encapsulated in love. Yet for most of us, to express such love was a fearsome thing. It was far easier to carry love in one's head and heart, or simply bask in the idea of it, rather than dare to write it down, or divulge such supposed sentimentality on to paper. Anyway, this new book would attempt, however inadequately, to tell something of that indescribable power which motivated our lives on earth, and of its effect on a group of people, living in a particular way. Woven through its pages would also be the attempt to tell of the extremes, the sacrifice and pain of love, its balance, its joy, its perfect freedom and its consummation . . .

Two gulls swooped over us, and God seemed to be saying: Look, if you continue to struggle in this way, you'll never write anything. Just loosen up, be yourself and fly a little. Don't make everything so unnecessarily complicated. Be simple, listen with your heart, and then write. Fussing is just a waste of time. You're not the subject of the book, I am. You're only a channel . . . so let go . . . and allow me to speak through you . . .

Pausing to admire the first violet of the year along the roadside, I thought how amazing it was that the tiniest thing could radiate so many facets of love. In fact, looking around, love was everywhere and in everything. Nevertheless, despite its manifestation in so many ways, I was aware that most of the world was obsessed with only one aspect – the physical aspect of love. And undoubtedly this was important and could not help but touch us all since our existence in this world had depended upon it . . .

Again I chuckled, for years earlier, when having a blood test, I had been asked a question which I had never been asked before. The enquiry, to do with the human, physical side of love, was posed in a very matter-of-fact, even casual sort of way and I had been acutely interested to note my response – and, indeed, the turmoil it had caused within. Medically, it was necessary to know whether I had, at any point in my life, been sexually active, 'Because if you haven't,' it was explained, 'we can eliminate one of the tests.' With great reluctance, I replied in the negative. 'So that's good, isn't it?' I declared. The nurse smiled, unaware of the ludicrousness of my sounding so calm, so devoid of any of that inner aggression I felt. Scratching a few notes in a book, she put down her pen. Meanwhile, my brain silently continued to fume, 'No, I haven't, but not because I'm strait-laced, and I expect that you're thinking I am, and that I've never wanted marital love, and that all nuns have some strange loathing of such things, and that I'm a person incapable of loving in that way or of ever having such feelings . . .'

For days, my mind weltered around in this manner. Actually, I am quite certain now that my excellent medical friend would never have entertained any of the opinions attributed to her. Certainly, she could not have known how much I had wanted to be loved, to fall in love, to be fulfilled by love, and especially in my youth, to be at one with a soul mate with whom I could travel through life. No, she would never have guessed that I was a born romantic and not at all the emotional iceberg ascribed to nuns, or that I, too, had longed to see the world through rose-coloured spectacles and touch the stars.

Shuna and I had reached the top of SOLI's right of way, where it met up with the single-track road which wound from the north to the eastern side of the isle. True to character, Shuna wanted to go on, though needing to return I twitched her about, and retracing our steps we ambled down the incline to the lower slopes of home.

Yes, I thought, my mind returning to Our Lady, people tended to think of her in that same stereotyped way as they thought of nuns, and on the whole to perceive her as the coldly untouchable. After all what could 'the Virgin of virgins', or any nun for that matter, know about marriage, or about love, or passion or sex? All I could think of was that, for the last forty years, my own life had been a total study of love. Surprisingly, perhaps I, and more than likely my SOLI Sisters too, were not, as many might imagine, people who had turned away from marriage in disgust, but were instead souls to whom marriage was so precious that we had offered it up to God. And, of course, 'cast your bread upon the waters and it will come back to you . . .' Personally, I had taken the risk of giving God what I most wanted, and amazingly, for me, nothing in the end had been lost but rather gained a hundredfold – in the spiritual sense, that was! Whatever anyone said, there were myriad outer facets of that inner, unspeakable glory of love that sadly many folk would never have the joy of knowing.

Striding along, my thoughts turned affectionately to a couple whom I had, in my priestly capacity, married, and I prayed that they would continue to grow in the knowledge that their love, as it matured into wholeness, was the one thing which would hold their journey on course. I prayed, too, that they would learn to love deeply and more deeply: learn to love the Lord their God, and in him to increasingly love and cherish each other; and more, that their same love would radiate outwards and embrace all those whom their lives touched.

So we, as religious, were particularly aware that there was a tendency to assume that monks and nuns were sterile people when, in fact, they were probably some of the most passionate on earth. Only a week earlier, I had been speaking to a middle-aged man on the telephone, who was asking if we would pray for him over a break-up with his girlfriend. 'You see,' he said, 'at my age I had thought that I would never have such feelings again – that was, until I met this lady. Now, and you're bound to understand, I'm seriously wondering if I'm meant to be a monk!' Laughingly, I had told him of a piece of wisdom I had learned from a Cowley Father who was, at one time, the confessor of the community in Devon to which I belonged. His words had both intrigued and pleased me and certainly made a lasting impression. Over a conversation at supper, Fr X had announced to the community at large that he felt the best religious were those who had first had the experience of falling in love! I can still feel the ripple of surprised shock that rolled around the table, and a strange contradictory surge of excitement rising within me.

Love was a gift that lay at the heart of our earthly nature as well as being the essence of our heavenly state. Physical love was natural and good – at least, I believed it to be good – and of course it was physical, natural people whom God called to follow him in the religious state. Yet, as monks and nuns, we were asked to make the extreme sacrifice of offering up the physical side of love for Love's own sake. Part of me still grappled with this and could not help feeling that within this mystery there was something of God's plan that we misinterpreted. Could it be that the essence of physical love would have a place in our ultimate heavenly journeying towards perfection? My basis for thinking so was the story of creation. The narrative told of God taking Eve from Adam, female from male and then reuniting them in a new way. Instead of there being only one human, suddenly there were two, who looked different, who did not think in quite the same way and yet who could be united and made perfect in one; and all this while still preserving their own identities. It was easy to understand the purposes of bodily union between male and female in this world, but I believed that the being 'made one' was definitely meant to include the mind and spirit too. And that through the power of love's binding, all those elements of body, mind and spirit should come together in one, in God, without any part being excluded. Truly, I thought, it would be incredible if all married couples were one day able to say together, with Our Lady, 'Be it unto me (us) according to thy word.'

In the early days of SOLI, I had the brave or maybe stupid idea that couples could in the future consecrate their lives together within our religious lifestyle. I believed that while still living a full married life, they could be united in one single offering to God. Now, I am doubtful if such a thing could ever happen, certainly here, in my lifetime. When a person with a true vocation relinquished the possibility of marriage in favour of the consecrated state of a life given wholly to God, there came with that offering a fulfilment which could not be described. For this to come about for a couple, they would need to have been entirely at one in body, mind and soul, and thus bound at one with God. However, as St Paul explained in a letter to the Corinthians, there was a dilemma with regard to this, for in marriage, he said, a person was naturally and rightly concerned for the things of the world and of how best to please a partner, whereas in the single state (and definitely in the religious state) one's concern was centred in the things of God and, by virtue of that fact, of how to please God! So it seemed to me that a perfect marital union, perfectly offered to God, in an imperfect world, would not be easy! Yet most of us knew that nothing was impossible, and would have to assent to the truth that God created Eve from Adam and that in their different male and female roles they were made to come together, to complement each other and become one in a bonding of love. Eventually, in a world made complete, no doubt that which had been lost would once more be found, souls united and couples and families made whole.

Pausing again while Shuna snuffled around, picking up some trail left by Kelpie, I thanked God for our life in this place and fell once more into comparing it to that of Our Lady. The girl Mary had walked as I walked today over the hills, she within whose womb love was swelling. She had carried, hidden within her, the incarnate God of the universe, he who had been conceived in so unfathomable a way. She had carried the Christ, the author of all being and of joy, and so became the great archetype mother of heaven and earth. She had given herself unconditionally to God, yet at the same time God had given her in marriage to Joseph, and who could say in what way? All we knew was that Joseph's hand had been placed in hers. Their wedlock, sacred to them only, was not our concern; all we needed to know was that Mary had given everything to God and that he had given himself to her. She had begun to fly. She had freely answered yes on behalf of us all, a yes which had been the beginning of the world's redemption.

The wings of love had carried Mary into the heart of the God who was Love, where probably the whole mystery of life would have been turned upside-down, and earth have been seen for what it was – a reflection of heaven. Sadly, such moments, of beholding, which should belong to us all, are rare. Plodding onwards, I remembered just one small occasion of my own.

Years before, when kneeling in the tiny oratory chapel that I had created in a loft-room of The Ness, I realized out of the blue that I had fallen in love. All that I had ever wanted, and in my youth had dreamed about, and given up, I knew in a strange way was in the process of being given back. All that had seemed lost was only the starting out on the real journey of receiving all. And most importantly, I knew that in the abandoning of 'self' I had found the freedom of being able to draw nearer to God, and that in a strange and deeper way he himself was drawing nearer to me. To merge into and become one with God, with our Christ, in this way, at whatever measure, was an indescribable thing. It was an experience of pure love, which carried within itself every other facet of love that humankind had ever known, and a million more. A seed had been sown in me, as it was sown by God in the hearts of us all. The world was meant to carry Love, as Love carried the world. Such love infused into the heart of humankind would surely burn away pride and, like the sunlight across the hill, transform the countenance of the earth. Maybe then all God's creatures, united and at one, would be able to sing the song of Mary. 'My soul doth magnify the Lord and my spirit hath rejoiced in God my Saviour.'

4

Love's Birth

It was difficult not to stare at the land and seascapes around me but I needed to concentrate harder on the driving. Guiding the car round the last few bends of the narrow road, I unexpectedly came upon them – three large caravans. Set back into the hillside so as to make each one more private, the dwellings were camouflaged by age, and meadow flowers of every colour gave them a welcoming air. Steering sharply to the left I wound up an incline, which brought me to a rough plateau of ground. Here I pulled on the brakes. Our vehicle, an old Volvo estate, was long and needed skilful manoeuvring to park it opposite the middle of the mobile homes. It took me a moment or two to get it tidily into place, then, switching off the engine, I dropped the ignition key into my pocket. The countryside around was sparsely populated and the views stunning. Looking up I noticed that a door had opened. A man and a woman, the owners of the accommodation, appeared and, stepping out on to the decking at the top of a wooden flight of steps, waved cheerily. Although this was to be my rented abode for the next week I had not expected so warm a welcome. Later my new friends, wishing me a happy few days, bade farewell. Then, trundling a suitcase, a bag of groceries and a laptop and printer up the steps, I settled everything around me and put on the kettle!

Sand, as the location was called, was a wonderful place of retreat situated on the west side of the Shetland Mainland, and my being there was only made possible by the generosity of Sylvia and Pauline, two of our SOLI Caim Members who themselves used it for a fortnight each year when visiting Shetland. When last in the isles, they had booked and paid for the caravan to be reserved for a week during the summer for my own use. Thrilled, I glanced around, deciding that the tiny abode was perfectly suited for the stepping-aside purpose which I hoped would enable me to detach myself sufficiently from SOLI so as to be able to take a look at our lifestyle from a different perspective. Normally, if I left Fetlar – which was rare, for I loved my home – it was to spend a couple of days at St Mahri's Hame with Sister Mary Aidan, and, delightful though my visits to Sister were, when there one was still immersed in SOLI. Hence, I had realized that every three or four years there was a need, for SOLI's sake as well as my own, to take a look at my spiritual family from the outside in! On this occasion I had arranged to do so with a particular job in mind, for I hoped to draft out our Rule, or as some religious communities would call it, our 'Plan of Life'. Yes, this tiny hermitage would be a place of blessing, and hopefully, this week, like the stable at Bethlehem, would also become a place of giving birth, of producing a Rule of life.

Knowing that I had set myself a daunting task, I was determined on this first evening to relax. So closing my eyes I leaned back into a chair by the window and inhaled the freedom of having time to take stock. Later, I would watch something lighthearted on the television – *The Vicar of Dibley*, perhaps – and tomorrow, away from the telephone and normal responsibilities of life at home, I would work unencumbered.

The pregnancy period of carrying the idea of SOLI had brought its physical weariness, sickness and emotional ups and downs. Notwithstanding, this beloved burden, safely protected and easily nurtured in the spiritual womb of the heart, had given me acute joy. Of course, to start with SOLI had been my secret and God's, and in part it was still a comfortable, cosy thought. However, the time had come when the necessary pains of giving birth to such a spiritual lovechild had to be faced.

The caravan's large picture window faced east, so I could not see the orb of sun as it dropped in a final flare of glory below the horizon. Nevertheless, its crimson glow spread long, watery fingers across the landscape. Yes, I thought, we called ourselves SOLI, a title which in itself always made one think of sun . . . of sunlight, of warmth . . . We called ourselves SOLI – the reflection of the glory of God, the reflection of Love himself.

Someone had once told me that SOLI was an old word with connotations describing the pagan sun-god, who was long ago worshipped by the Vikings in these dark northern shores. Whether this was true or not, the name echoed many things, including the word 'solitary'. Obviously, too, the letters were an abbreviation of our own title of dedication, the Society of Our Lady of the Isles. Yet still I loved the interpretation of the 'symbol of the sun', feeling that it was not by chance we were called to be SOLI. Though to be named SOLI or sun, the symbol of the reflection of God, of the mirror of God, of the light of God, was an awesome responsibility, for the imagery it repre-sented had to show, and could only do so when a life was, and continued to be, fully and generously given – in love.

The sun, of course, had many moods. Cloud-strewn, it lay concealed. At other times it was tearful; in mist it appeared soft and mysterious and on a summer's day there was great joy in its warmth. Yet without doubt at sunrise and at sunset it was glorious . . . and we, God's children, were called to radiate its reflection, to radiate the Sun of Righteousness, to radiate the Spirit of Love generated in us and, as Rosemary would have said, 'to be shining ones'. Nothing mattered more than this, for if such sunlight were not at the heart of our life, with all the wonder and the freedom 'to be' which came from it, then whatever we did, however we did it, whatever lifestyle we followed or rules we adhered to, they were of no account – at least, not in so far as our calling was concerned. Nor were any of the extraneous or in-built aspects of the traditional or modern methods of the religious life worth anything, if we had not first learned of love – the sort of love that gave to the uttermost. And it was this 'uttermost' which I expected of every SOLI member. Unfortunately, such commitment was not easily given or under-stood and, strangely, for some it might even seem too simple! Nevertheless, having this quality was essential, especially to a group of religious, for it was the one thing which would bind such a family into the entity that God wanted it to be. Yes, the whole spirit of what we were about was Love, and everything else would shine from that.

The next morning at breakfast, sitting in front of the same window, I determined how best to fashion our lifestyle into words. During those early, solitary years of living at The Ness, I had thought a great deal about the kind of life that SOLI would live in Shetland when God sent others to join me. Fascinatingly, before setting off to come here, I had found some forgotten old notes headed: 'The Object of the Rule and its Observance'. Spreading them across the table I bit into a piece of toast and read the first sheet curiously.

'Our Rule, the Discipline of Love,' it said, 'is contained and summed up in one simple word – Love; for it is only within the discipline of Love that we are safe and able to find the perfect freedom to be . . .'

Flipping through a number of the tired-looking pages, I saw with astonishment how I had underlined the word 'freedom' many times over. In every chapter, love in a strange way equalled freedom – the freedom 'to be' who God had, and was, creating us to be. Finishing my breakfast, I washed up, said Mattins and then switched on the laptop. Yes, I thought, one of the purposes of any rule was to provide boundaries within which we could abide, be safe, schooled – and not least – set free!

With hands poised above the keyboard, I wondered how best to begin. Well, I thought, an example drifting into my mind, what about taking a child, born into a home in which he was greatly loved. Because he was loved, it went without saying that he would be kept within safe confines for his own sake, and that within those confines with their necessary constraints, there would be security, a happy environment and the freedom to grow. Yes . . . and this was how it was with SOLI, I decided excitedly. To engender spiritual growth it was necessary to have a set of rules in place, for both support and protection, rules which hopefully (for we all have the freedom of choice) would set us free from any of the disharmonies which could arise among a group of people living at fairly close quarters. Contention was something that could so easily arise within any group, whether religious or not, especially a collection of women. God seemed to toss folk together, with such different temperaments and sometimes from differing backgrounds, countries and cultures, people whom he called together to bind in comm-*unity*, to be a family of people *at one* with each other. So rules – or in the case of a religious society a clearly spelt out Rule – were necessary.

In the Christian life, and certainly for SOLI, it was Love who built those supports, those protective walls of the Rule; and he our Guardian and our Guide built them with the bricks of his own life, and with his Holy Word. Within the Gospels were found Love's own commands, which were his laws for us, not ours. When founding the Franciscans, St Francis had impelled his brethren to take the Holy Gospel of Christ as their Rule, and equally for us, the life of Christ was our example and pattern.

Mid-morning I stopped to make a cup of coffee, and staring out of the window at a view now dotted with sheep I reflected on my morning's work. Mary and Joseph had known about rules

too, for under the Jewish law they had followed a decree requiring them to journey to Bethlehem. Come to think of it, the shepherds keeping watch over their flocks had also followed instructions . . . They, in their response to the words of God's angelic messenger, had complied, even to the degree of leaving their sheep. And indeed, if the shepherds' submission had led them to the wonder of finding the Christ Child, so ours too could bring similar, if undue, reward. Standing up, I muddled in the cupboard, found a tea biscuit and sat down again. As seekers of the truth, we too were sometimes asked by God to do things that seemed contradictory, things which tested our faith. Those abandoned sheep of the shepherds would, I am sure, have been kept safe, in exactly the same way in which all those good things we thought we were relinquishing, for the sake of following a bidding or in the keeping of a rule, were likewise kept safe. In fact our Rule, in itself, was a stronghold built by God. It was a sheepfold with a shepherd who was Christ, whose life we imitated and whose voice we obeyed. SOLI's Rule, then, was a stronghold where we could grow in the freedom of God's will for us, until ultimately, in the joy of his presence, we were able to 'go in and out and find pasture'. So a Rule was not simply to provide us with a set of regulations, as many imagined, but rather to guide us forward as we sought to love and serve God. It was to help us know how to follow our shepherd who was Love and, in that following, to ourselves become love.

Returning to the computer for an hour before saying the noon-hour Office and preparing lunch I continued to work. All my life I had searched, looking for the one thing which made sense of everything else, the answer which would put the whole mystery of life into a nutshell, and I had found it – found that which was pivotal; found that which lay at the heart of all those things which many people thought were the be-all and end-all of their existence; all those things which we humans called 'my life', 'my vocation', 'my work', 'my gifts', things which we were adept at basing an entire lifetime on: good things, Christian things – nursing, teaching, preaching, mission . . . and a million more. Slowly, however, I had learned that unless all these callings carried Love at their centre, they would never grow to their potential.

Mary had risked all in saying 'yes' to Love, and in her carrying of him in her womb she had made it possible for the same Love, our God, to give himself to the world. Subsequently, we had been enabled to carry him at the centre of our own being, and in turn to become God-bearers – Love-bearers. In a sense, I suppose, we had become centres of a spiritual universe, which permitted everything, from the smallest detail of our life to all those things we were called to accomplish, to become spin-offs of Love. Because I felt so strongly about this, it frustrated me when people came up with a mind-blowing, spiritual idea they had discovered, or some spiritual conclusion about the using of their gifts, or some central objective upon which they were now going to base every thought, word and deed. All such certainties, all our training and talents were important, of course, and if related to love were good, though tended to throw life out of kilter if they themselves became the centre. It appeared to me, as I sat at the caravan table, that however much Christians stated their understanding of the overriding significance of love, some mistakenly regarded it as only one of many aspects of their spirituality. As said, all things appertaining to our spiritual good were in their differing degrees important, yet were they crucial enough upon which to anchor the whole of one's Christian life? Like satellites around the sun, our gifts and skills, our offerings great or small were only spin-offs from that great and mysterious orb of God.

Love was the Sun, and the only entity which was pivotally essential to life. For myself, I had found that when love was at the centre, everything else automatically spun into a true orbiting course. To place something else at the heart of our life would be like trying to position the earth or one of the other planets at the centre of the Milky Way! Mary had borne and brought forth the Christ, and afterwards had presented him to the world, so allowing the Sun of Righteousness to take his course through the skies of human life. I prayed that his brightness might again cast warmth and radiance over the earth, and that the earth might take heed and adore him.

Glancing again at my old notes I felt pleased that my feelings about our vocation had not changed, and that within our SOLI framework we needed to have this 'spin-off' structure, so that everything appertaining to the life, whether it were prayer, work or recreation, spun from and was 'of Love'. By inference, it was plain to me that our whole Rule was of Love, therefore making prayer the dialogue of Love, reading and study the enlightenment of Love, the Divine Office the worship and praise of Love. And with regard to our vows of Poverty, Chastity and Obedience, they became the poverty of Love, the obedience of Love and the purity of Love. One could go on, stressing the real purpose of the Rule and knowing that, without Love, all those things so integrally related to the body, mind and spirit were of little account. Our Lord, who was Love, was our Sun, and we ourselves, despite all our baggage, were all satellites of Christ, and thereby, sustained and illuminated by him.

This concept in its simplicity was of paramount importance to me. Yet, as said, I knew that although love was so obviously there for everyone to receive and give, generally speaking it was not thought of as the focal point of our existence. Come to think of it, when mentioning the subject I often heard myself doing so in such a way as not to sound sentimental, and often felt as though I was inviting people to think, 'Oh dear, she's talking about love again!' Yet love was God. Love was the cherishing, nourishing sustainer, shown to us tangibly and epitomized in Christ. I had touched him, he had entered my being, and he was at the heart of the SOLI that lay buried in me and in that group of people gathered about me . . . Now, after Mary's example, we were to show him forth. Joy gripped me. We, SOLI, were to show forth that same babe born in a stable.

Earlier, looking out over the receding land to the sky and sea, life had felt good. At this moment, in this tiny place, this womb, this stable and place of being, I felt uplifted. God had called SOLI, as he calls us all, not because we were particularly able or clever, but simply to be channels of himself. My first day here, already half over, was racing away and it was time to say the noon-hour Office.

Laying aside the day's work and looking around for my breviary, I thought how significant it was that I had eight days here at the caravan to work on the principles of our life. Interestingly, Mary and Joseph had had eight days before the official naming of their Son, and now for me too there was this time of clarification, though in my case of formulating and identifying the principles of our life. I opened the book. Yes, within eight days, the lifestyle of SOLI was to be identified, pulled out and drafted on to paper in the form of a Rule. Like a newborn babe it would be fragile, and as a document ill-defined, though dear to me despite its wizened form. Later, we would need to nourish it into growth and beauty, into health and strength, so that ultimately God's plan could be fulfilled.

Typing out a final sentence I switched off the computer and pulled open a partially drawn curtain, letting in a flood of sunlight. This love, which was God's command, had been imbibed by so many before us; recently, it had pleased me to read that St Benedict and St Aelred had both said that their monasteries were 'schools of love'. Yes, we also had above all other things to learn, with the same humbleness as they, our Lord's first and greatest commandment. This meant giving ourselves up to that which would carry us through all our stumbling, through every confine of our mortal lives and into eternity, allowing it to transform each aspect of our lives, so that everything belonged to and became Love . . . Already, Love was giving our lifestyle its true dimension. And that, I breathed, is the spirit of SOLI – that was our Rule.

SOLI's framework for each day

A hermitage is the nun's individual home or cell, where the Offices are often said solitary.

Weeks 1 and 3	
DAWN-HOUR OFFICE/PRIME	Hermitage
Breakfast	Hermitage
Prayer/Work/Study	Hermitage/Chapel/ or wherever one is working
MATTINS	Hermitage
Prayer/Work/Study	Arranged location as above
NOON-HOUR OFFICE	Hermitage
Lunch	Hermitage
VESPERS	Chapel, 2.00 p.m.
Silent Prayer	Chapel
EUCHARIST	Chapel
Prayer/Work/Study	Arranged location
Supper	Hermitage
Free time	
COMPLINE	Hermitage/Chapel
Free time	

Weeks 2 and 4
Mattins, Silent Prayer and Eucharist are said in chapel at 10.00 a.m. and Vespers is said in the hermitage.

5

Love Presented

After moving into our wooden, boat-shaped house on the cliff, I had at first shared the roof space with Sister Mary Clare. She had chosen to use the east end for her hermitage and I the west. The west was lovely with its pointed window looking out over the bay of Tresta, though being open-plan it sometimes proved draughty. Contrariwise, the east end, which was the same size in area, had been chopped into three smaller rooms, and in the winter this was cosier. Between the two there was a passage and bathroom, so the whole design worked splendidly. Sadly, after a year or two of living there, Mary Clare became increasingly dispirited with the eremitical direction in which SOLI was moving, and finally, though not without deep reluctance, we agreed that she should be seconded by SOLI to help with a more socially active project in Orkney.

In due course, accepting the inevitable that Sister Mary Clare would not be returning to Fetlar in the near future, I moved into the eastern side of the roof area, and found it both warmer and quieter. Certainly, it was a relief to be out of the firing line of our southwesterly prevailing wind, which on certain days in the winter had to be experienced to be believed. Later, we reallocated the west side as a hermitage for visiting SOLI Members, though preferably not in the winter! The western room also became a favourite place for community gatherings and an ideal spot for interviews, or having a cuppa with anyone who wished to speak privately. Meanwhile, at the opposite side, which was something of a rabbit warren, I had now made a cosy sitting room off the galley kitchen. This led through a curtained doorway into a small office-cum-study, and from there one could step into the gallery room. The gallery room, an even smaller, cell-like area, resembled a tiny anchorhold. Inside was just enough space for a bed, a bedside table, a chair and a piece of furniture in which to keep clothes. I painted the area in white silk emulsion, which not only gave it a clean, uncluttered air but made it especially pleasing when the sun, shining through the skylight, caused the red cover on the bed to reflect its light off the walls, so turning the whole room roseate. Best of all, this little cell, with its pointed, beamed ceiling, had a second, unusually shaped door which led out on to a narrow balcony that overhung the chapel, hence the name 'gallery room'. The whole room was of enormous pleasure to me, especially since I was able, so easily, to slip through on to the gallery to say the Divine Office, pray or read.

On the gallery that Sunday morning I lingered a while longer, enjoying Jean's music, for down below she was practising her voluntary for the next day's Sung Mass. The organ, tucked immediately under the gallery, was out of sight, but the strains of what I guessed was Bach rose upward. Jean, also our choir mistress, kept us all in order, though our choir, now somewhat depleted, had become a real 'little band and lowly'. We felt the lack of Rosemary's and Frances's powerful voices, as also Sister Mary Clare's ability to sing the contralto parts. Sighing, I stood up and turned to the door. It was easy to understand how God needed different types of people with different gifts and leanings. Sister Mary Clare declared that her propensity was much more towards a 'practical, caring vocation'. Even so, her departure had brought sadness. If only she had been able to continue along a path down which, we were convinced, SOLI was more and more being drawn, and which proffered so much joy to the rest of us.

Turning briefly towards the altar once more I prayed that, at least, I might catch something of the substance of our vocation on to paper, something in addition to the draft Rule I had written. In other words, I wanted to produce a more general booklet for all who showed interest and asked questions, something which they could read and, hopefully, grasp in a nutshell.

The altar stood at the centre of the octagonal-shaped chapel, and placed at its centre stood a ciborium, covered by a white veil. The vessel contained the consecrated elements of the bread and wine – the Blessed Sacrament, which indicated the presence of Our Lord Jesus Christ. As always, I found strength from this, the great source of all strength and, today, unexpected inspiration. Perhaps, I decided, I could draw a diagram or find some similar way of explaining the life, so that everyone would understand its relevance in a glance. Genuflecting, I turned back to the door and, passing through the gallery room into the study, made for my desk. Yes, maybe it was possible to show what I meant in diagram form, or even, perhaps, in a set of diagrams . . . Sitting down, I pulled out a sheet of paper and pencil. More than anything, I wanted people to understand the simplicity and the joy of our life. Comparatively few would be drawn in the direction of the religious life themselves – and there was no reason why they should – but at least, if I managed it, this might give them some glimmering of the nature of our calling and of its viability.

Completing the diagrams more quickly than expected, I scratched a few notes around them. And so it was that the following explanation of SOLI appeared, one, which I had wanted to call 'SOLI at a glance', though, as it turned out, it became SOLI in two or three glances!

SOLI

Introduction

On the surface, SOLI may appear as though nothing much is going on, though, based on fact, a lot of things are happening. Let me explain – to my mind, a religious house such as we have been asked to form, is a living organism in which there is constant growth and movement, and this is precisely why a diagram of the spiral has been chosen to symbolize who and what we represent as a spiritual family.

What I am saying is that God is building us into a kind of power-house that generates both energy and light from the source of his own being – love. In other words, he has called us as individual channels and as a religious family to be catalysts of himself, who is Love.

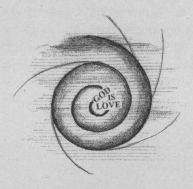

As already said in the draft Rule:

We are called to be SOLI – a reflection to others, to the world, if you like, of the glory of God, and it must show, though will only do so when a life is fully and generously given in love.

Interestingly, we are told that there is a spiral in everything, and I believe that this is particularly true within each one of us as spiritual human beings. For myself, I increasingly feel that the power of God pulsates from the centre of such a spiral, and that revolving outwards, the light and energy of his love comes first into the soul, second into the mind, and third into and through the body. In this way, he who is the light and energy at the centre of our beings propels each one of us, if we will, into wholeness. Slowly he illuminates us into reflections of his own glory. For me, and very importantly, this same pattern is to be found within our religious lifestyle as a community. I will attempt to show with diagrams what I mean.

What I would most like to get over is how naturally every aspect of our life falls into place, yet, paradoxically – because life is about living, from which, of course, comes movement – none of the aspects are kept rigidly separated from each other but instead merge, in a spiral-like movement. Indeed, within these aspects of soul, mind and body, which are all integrally related and able to become one with each other, are carried the smaller, subdivided rudiments of daily life. And here, in a balance of ebb and flow, comes the growth spoken of.

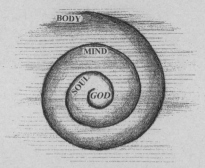

The Soul Centre or The Soul Illumined

To me, it seems that the light of God's love illuminates SOLI's life from what I will call its soul centre, which is, of course, our place of communion with God. It is a place which is sacred and where we are drawn into the immersion of Love's own light. This union with Love, with God himself, generally happens in our times of profound silence and contemplation and in our receiving of Christ within ourselves at the Eucharist; in other words, at those times when we deliberately place ourselves at the source. Nevertheless, it is possible, on other occasions for a person who is familiar with the soul centre to move into the light of the contemplation of God, at the busiest of moments. Physically, the chapel, or some other place set aside, often one's individual hermitage, represents this sanctum of union with God, and this is why such areas of our life must always be kept sacrosanct, both corporately and individually – hence the reason for our insistence that, as a community, we should never use the chapel for unnecessary chatter. Both physically and spiritually, this central place (wherever it is) needs to be accessible and used entirely for God's purpose and as a place to be with God in a special way. We can all become 'up-tight' when we feel cut off or when we

get pile-ups of unnecessary intrusion – the kind that throws us out of step, and holding us back seemingly separates us from this special space. We have a deep need, and sometimes starve (if that is not putting it too strongly) for the nourishment that this central and most important core of our vocation gives. And we need it in order to be sustained in our ability to function as God wills in all those other spiralled-out areas of our life, that he has called us to incorporate. So this soul centre is our place of 'being', and as I frequently tire people by saying: If we are to succeed in our vocation, it is imperative we take time to 'be' there in that place with God, for, always, what we 'do' on the outer edges of our life comes from who we have allowed God to make us in that inner sanctuary.

The mind illumined

The wondrously concentrated source of God's love at the soul centre of our life then spins outwards to enlighten the area of the mind. In this place comes our participation in the corporate prayer of the whole Church of God; that is, in our recitation of the Divine Office. Also included in this mind area comes our meditation, spiritual reading and study, and all those things that add up to the praise and reflection of God, in and through our minds.

The body illumined

The light that floods outwards from the centre of SOLI's life – that is, through our soul's communion with God and then through the enlightenment of our minds – further spirals outwards into and through our physical bodies. Some of the saints are said to have had countenances that shone. We also are called to be saints and, with them, to be 'shining ones', and this will be so if we are true witnesses of something as significant as our ever deepening relationship with God. Anyway, I am sure that if we are deeply soul-centred in God – in Love – and enlightened by him in our minds, however simply (and the simple people are sometimes the most enlightened) then physically, our bodies will manifest his light in the seemingly mundane area we call our work: that is, in such things as our hospitality, our necessary jobs in the house, office or garden, etc. Certainly, all these outer things can be transformed, within the physical realm of our earthly life, and so become a glorifying of, a witness of, and a shining out from God. So, in effect, everything will then become a part of our union, our relationship with God, a part of our being, in Love, and our 'being in Love' in turn, will become – our life.

WORK & SERVICE

GOD

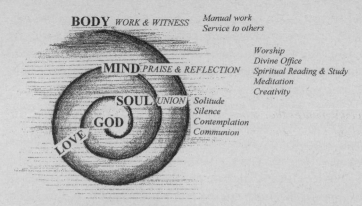

BODY *WORK & WITNESS*   *Manual work*
                         Service to others

MIND *PRAISE & REFLECTION*   *Worship*
                              Divine Office
                              Spiritual Reading & Study
SOUL *UNION* *Solitude*   *Meditation*
              Silence   *Creativity*
GOD   *Contemplation*
              Communion
LOVE

SOLI – at a glance!

Note: *Like work and prayer, rest and recreation are also an essential part of our growth, which covers all areas of the spiral of body, mind and soul. They are part of the overall rhythm and balance of who we are, and are becoming.*

The bell on the landing jangled, which meant that lunch was ready. Finishing off the sentence, I gathered the text and drawings tidily together and hurried to meet Sybil, who was already halfway up the stairs with a tray. Irritated with myself for not being quicker off the mark, I received the meal with apologies and took it along to the nyook (the Shetland name I gave to my small sitting room).[1]

While eating, my mind ran on, still thinking of the concept of the spiral. In SOLI's beginnings I had used a wheel to symbolize what was growing. Yet, over the years that rather tight circular illustration had evolved into something more. It had spun into the living, freer shape of the spiral, into that which emanated the warmth and love of God from its centre. Indeed, the convolutions of the spiral, unlike the initial 'wheel' circles (which admittedly moved round and forward) were not confined, but rather living organisms, made up of people in whom was growth, movement and merging. They were people, living souls, who were channels of love, soaking up love and giving out love – the love of him who, at the heart of our life, was love. The motion of this love within the spiral concept was like a current, perpetually ebbing and flowing.

After the meal I returned to the study to add a few more thoughts and an additional diagram to the morning's work, and later, since the day was what we called a hermit day, I slipped again to the gallery to say Vespers, alone.

Earlier, in chapel, the vibration of Jean's music had caused me to consider life's amazing rhythm and symmetry, and to realize afresh that in order to live a full, joyous life one needed to be in alignment with its shape and movement – with God's amazing plan. From the balcony I could see across the chapel and through the 20-foot-high window opposite. A jagged line of boulders with rosa rugosa in full bloom splayed over them, and in the field beyond, whiter than white, newly shorn sheep ambled in and out of the view. The ewes glanced anxiously around, searching for their now well-endowed and comparatively grubby-looking lambs, which all appeared ridiculously larger than their clipped mothers. The grass was green and lush, the sky flashed with bird wings, and all in all, whether in roses, grass, stones, sky or birds, there was harmony. In his adult life, Christ had used such symbolic images to illustrate his message from God, and, I am sure, must have rejoiced that in everything there was inner meaning. Glancing across at the statue of Our Lady on the eastern wall of the chapel, I thought of how she and St Joseph had also used symbols. They had carried their doves or perhaps pigeons to the temple as an offering, in their presenting of God's Son to the world. Had they held the birds out for the child to see, and would his eyes have taken in the fluttering feathers of those tiny miracles of being which were to be sacrificed for him? At only a few weeks old he would still have been looking considerably new, perhaps not yet perfectly rounded; a bit like SOLI, I thought. Yet, so gently, Simeon the old man had taken the child in his arms and, holding him up, had presented God's own sacrifice to the world.

Of course, Anna, the prophetess, was there too, she who for most of her 84 years had lived a hermit-type lifestyle – a calling which had prohibited any leaving of the temple. Yet on that day had come her life's crowning, for the old lady had stood beside Simeon to receive the Christ . . . In a way, I supposed, we Sisters were not unlike her, in that we did not leave our SOLI base excepting for some good reason. Obviously, too, like us, such a precept would have been dictated by a Rule of life, though, again, I accentuate that such maxims were only credible when they were in place to set free, rather than to bind. Within our own calling we had discovered that there had to be balance and harmony, discipline and flexibility. Indeed, for us, flexibility was an essential ingredient of the life, since things that were too rigid, especially Rules, broke! Also, it went without saying that without such an input of flexibility along with our discipline I could not have taken the week at the caravan or made my monthly visits to St Mahri's Hame. And it went without saying that without a degree of flexibility there would be no opportunities to visit family, have a change of scene or a special time of rest and recreation, although for SOLI such times away frequently turn into busmen's holidays.

On one such occasion, the autumn after Rosemary died, I had taken a week with her sister and brother-in-law – Joan and David, who were Members of the Caim, living in North Yorkshire. This particular year I had agreed to preach at a Sunday Eucharist at St Gregory's Minster, and to take a service of the renewal of wedding vows for David and Joan in their village church. Other than that, I was free to spend the rest of that week on my own. My hosts had, over many years, renovated their old cottage and its outhouses into a beautiful home. Part of it, over the garages and with views over the garden, had been made into a self-contained flat for their guests. This I always enjoyed, for it was a place where one could come and go at will. On that occasion I had, as usual, taken some work to do, though over and above that, Sister Mary Aidan had challenged me to design a logo for SOLI – something, she said, that incorporated the spiral! Sadly, however, my initial enthusiasm was quickly to wane, since with no amount of doodling was I able to catch the essence of what I wanted. Unsuccessful, to the time I left, I binned my efforts.

Towards the end of that time away, Joan and David had insisted they give me a 'proper day off' and suggested we drive to the ruined Yorkshire priory of Mount Grace. Instantly trans-ported back through a dozen years or more, I could hear Rose-mary telling me how her relatives had taken her to that same 'wonderful place . . . It's just your sort of thing,' she had enthused. Painted in such glowing colours, her descriptions came vividly to mind, as did her words: 'Mother, you simply must go there one day, you'd love it . . . The monks, you know, each had their own little hermitage-cell with a private walled garden, and one of the hermitages has been reconstructed . . .'

Unlike other religious who lived in common, I knew that the Carthusians of Mount Grace had lived as hermits, each occupy-ing a hermitage and only coming together at a prescribed time for worship in the church. How super, I rejoiced, and perhaps even providential, that I too had been given an invitation to visit the place. It felt almost as though Rosemary herself was propelling me in that direction. Certainly, I had found it surprising that she had been so moved by Mount Grace, particularly since she was so much more geared to a communal, active lifestyle. However, God works in mysterious ways, as we know, and later I discovered that there were many similarities between the Carthusians of Mount Grace and what we envisaged for SOLI. Even the monks' ancient timetable compared, in part, with ours. Still, I found it thought-provoking how Rosemary had been so adamant . . . though one is apt to find, on numerous occasions in life, that the persons who seem least likely to lead us in a certain direction are exactly the people who prove instrumental in getting us there!

The day I was taken to Mount Grace was one of those unforgettable ones when the hills and villages of the North Yorkshire countryside were stippled in sunlight. Along the way we stopped to have lunch in an old pub before going on to the priory. Arriving, I found that Rosemary had been right: There was something incredibly 'encompassing' about the place, something with which I felt totally at home. Moreover, with growing certainty I felt that I had been meant to go and that the whole air of the ruin spoke to me. Its past spoke of our future and of the essence of our spirituality: remarkably, all that had been, in that monastery, was still the prime constituent of what was to come for SOLI. For an hour I wandered around, pausing in and around the reconstructed monk's cell and its garden plot, savouring the tangible as well as those echoes of its elusive past. The surrounding woodland gave the vale an enclosed feeling of sanctuary. The ruined

Statue of Our Lady, Mount Grace Priory

church was small, and with its tower still intact bore witness to an ageless God. The stone cross, which had been placed where the high altar might long have stood, told of an enduring faith. On closer examination of the cross, I found that it was also a statue of Our Lady, as a young girl, holding the Christ Child out in her arms and, like Simeon, presenting him to the world.

The gallery door behind me creaked open an inch or two and I turned and looked around. As I expected, a furry grey head and then a body squeezed through the gap. 'Are you ravenous again?' I whispered. To my surprise and before I had the chance to obligingly jump to attention, Mooskit turned back and, stretching out a long paw, pulled the door further ajar and disappeared, abandoning, I suspected, his momentary fancy for food. Hearing him jump on to my bed in the next room, I knew that he had opted to cut his losses, in favour of comfort!

Jean had long vacated her organ bench, leaving the chapel to the hushed silence of heaven's vibratos. Standing, and then leaning over the gallery rail, I once more considered our own statue of Our Lady on the far wall. It had been Jean who had brought it as a birthday gift for me from the States years before. Two foot high, it was wooden and was of Mary sheltering a huddle of children under her cloak. All at once, I could see her carrying the babe, the Christ, again at the Presentation with the same cloak-like garment folded around and encompassing him. How sheltered and loved he must have felt and how loved we were, encompassed and kept safe by a power that no words could convey . . . Thank you, Lord,' I whispered. Such love was like a great, gentle sea . . . it was like a dark spiralling movement of energy swallowing one into itself, into the alpha and omega of all things.

6

Love Found

Winding up the right of way to St Mahri's Hame, I peered at the house on the treeless hill to see if there were any signs of Sister Mary Aidan. A couple of moments later she emerged from a doorway and waved. The journey between our dwellings on Fetlar and St Mahri's Hame was beautiful, and usually took about three hours, which included the two ferry crossings. Living in Shetland, we thought little of such a trip unless the weather was rough! Although, having said that, I had developed a love–hate relationship with the Shetland wind, and on occasions even enjoyed a storm. It could be awe-inspiring, of course, to watch the sea raging around the isles, though increasingly, as time went

St Mahri's Hame

by, I disliked being tossed about on its surface, and today, with winter imminent, it had not been good.

Emerging from the car I was given a huge bear hug from Sister and very quickly, in order to get out of the wind, we unloaded the various items I had brought for her. Everything around us rattled, our veils and habits billowed and flapped and the wind, being no respecter of persons, snatched and tore at everything in its path. 'Hold on to the hatchback,' I yelled, 'and I'll carry things to and fro.'

'Mmm, something smells good!' I remarked, as we bundled the last bits of baggage in through the porch. Barney and Pippin, the two cats, with lunch obviously in mind too, threaded in and around our feet, getting thoroughly in the way.

'Yes, lunch is ready. Would you like to eat now? How was the journey?'

'A bit choppy, to say the least, and yes, just what I need – I'm famished, and could be ready for a meal as soon as you like.'

'You had a lovely time away, I take it,' she went on, hanging over the cooker and almost vanishing in a cloud of steam.

'Oh yes, I've lots to tell you, especially about Mount Grace.'

'Great. Did you manage to design our SOLI logo?'

After lunch we settled with a cup of coffee in the sitting room, where a picture window extended almost to the floor. Relaxing on the couch, able to gaze out across the expansive views and sea loch to the hills beyond, gave great pleasure, as did the perpetual Shetland sheep, loitering in and out of the frame. The loch, or the 'voe' as we called it up here, curved around the house and could be seen from other windows too. In the early morning and evening its waters were often a feast of colour, though that afternoon they were a ruffled grey.

Sister, in her Novice Guardian capacity, wanted to talk to me about updating our present process for those who thought God might be calling them to test their vocation. We had learned, in our enthusiasm of welcoming women to SOLI, that we must carefully guard against any would-be aspirant building up false expectations about her future, either as a Sister or a Companion. Consequently, each step of the way was a slow one, and often we needed to be brutally honest with regard to expectations on both sides. People read my books and used our visitor accommodation throughout the summer months for retreat-type holidays and, of course, the life here at that time of the year could seem idyllic and appealing. Unfortunately, it could also tempt certain souls with happy thoughts of escapism! Bearing this in mind, we had learned that before anyone joined us, in the official sense, they needed to be fully aware that contrary to what they might have anticipated, the vocation was, in fact, quite tough. Indeed, such a religious calling would not have been worth much without periods of difficulty and stretching. Since the first necessary requirement for a person was as simple as whether she could cope with a Shetland winter or not, we asked people to come to live alongside us for a month during the winter, before ever attempting to enter any kind of process of discernment. And even when an invitation to a candidate had been issued, it did not necessarily mean that a vocation with SOLI was a foregone conclusion. There would still be many questions to be asked and practicalities to be ascertained. The first real question was whether she was willing to enter a way of life which would invariably change her way of doing things. This, of course, could prove a hard nut to crack, though in one of Sister Mary Aidan's papers she quoted the great monastic truth that such a life was to be lived joyfully, rather than endured! So, ultimately, anyone wishing to test her vocation with SOLI needed to show early signs of humility and patience, and also to possess a capacity for joy!

Probably the hardest thing for any beginner to learn was to trust those in whose care God had placed her. Thus, obedience, which in itself was a loving compliance with what was asked, was the main promise a Novice made, though it could often seem the most difficult. Nevertheless, early, joyful obedience had helped all of us to plug a few unexpected chinks in ourselves, and thereby to keep steadily afloat. So for the Aspirant and Novice, the facing up to a few truths about herself enabled her to start at the beginning, which was a good and important place, and not at all, as some people imagined, one of instant brain-washing. Neither SOLI nor any other religious house I knew would ever do that. Instead, this early part of our process of discernment was a working, sharing and living with more experienced people, and the whole exercise, the beginning of a pilgrimage towards freedom and abandonment into God.

Aspirants, like children or the beginners to any life, could be self-willed, and although we found nothing wrong with having character – for it was often a healthy sign – we also knew that it could on the rare occasion be destructive. Strength of will was only good when channelled by goodness, which meant, for us, by the God of all Goodness himself. We had also noticed that many who offered their lives to him within a religious community laid enormous stress on how much they were offering, when really, if they but knew it, most religious communities were probably more interested in how little the Aspirant felt she was offering! Therefore, we maintained that some feeling of lowliness was imperative – that it was not so much what one had gained before one's entry into the life which was important, but rather the fact of knowing how small our offering was to God. This all sounded very conflicting, and in no way implied that God did not call strong people into the religious life, for without a doubt he called giants. However, at such an early, novitiate stage of a vocation no one could be exactly sure of what God was sculpting out of a soul, and therefore any assumptions or preconceived ideas and plans were often a waste of energy. So it was that a Novice with a true calling soon learnt that the religious life was an enormous act of faith, a real casting off of vainglory. Really, the criteria for any of us was that of reaching outwards from Love and, in his love, into a further radiating out of that same love to all around, be they near or far. Christ, said that we must be born again and certainly the entry into the religious life was exactly that. It was a spiralling back to base to start again, but this time in order to revolve outwards on a new level.

An hour or so later we stopped to say Vespers in the chapel, up in the loft. Earlier, on an occasion when Sister was south, in Aberdeen for a three-day hospital visit, and I was left at St Mahri's Hame house-and-cat-sitting, I had built a stairway from the hall up through the trapdoor into the loft. With some trepidation Sister had agreed to this idea before setting off, although for the obvious reason that she would have deterred me from such a ploy I had gone into few details regarding my plans. Nevertheless, convinced that she would like the stairs, I swiftly worked out the measurements and ordered and collected the pieces of wood. Quickly, and with an increasing number of bumps, bruises and scratches to my anatomy, the stairway began to take shape. What I had also refrained from telling Sister was how I hoped to emulsion the loft, lay a spare piece of carpet and generally turn the roof space into an upstairs chapel. However, her eventual delight at the final transformation surpassed all my hopes and was worth every moment of secrecy and slogging. Most of us like surprises – nice ones, that is – and Sister was thrilled and creatively replete! So, there in that tiny chapel, the Blessed Sacrament of the consecrated body and blood of Our Lord Jesus Christ was reserved on the altar, and from that time had represented the outward sign of his presence in the house, in a most wonderful way. The great mystery of the Eucharist was our greatest privilege, and of this words could not tell, for the consecrated bread and wine was Christ in the midst of us, uniting us with himself, and with each other.

After Vespers, Sister Mary Aidan leaned towards me, saying that she would go downstairs and put on the kettle. 'D'you mind if I stay for a few more moments?' I murmured back.

'Of course not,' she replied, squeezing past me and rounding the banister at the top of the narrow stairway.

Continuing to sit on the low stool, my mind still full of the afternoon's discussion about future Aspirants, I prayed that we might get everything right with regard to our plans for the training of Aspirants and Novices. Human souls were precious, and whether our Aspirants were meant to persevere in the life as we lived it or not, it behoved us to show a deep and loving regard for them. We had always stated that no one needed to feel they had made a mistake in testing their vocation with SOLI, whichever direction it took. If they had moved positively through the process we had in place, as though across stepping stones, we were sure that it would lead them on towards a deeper commitment to God, either within SOLI or in whatever else he, in his wisdom, had planned for them.

In the silence my thoughts turned to the boy Jesus, lost and then found in the temple. He, too, had reached out to God, in his maturing into the life of the spirit, and at 12 years old had sought to perceive the truth. He had asked questions relating to his own unique vocation. This, too, was what we expected of our Novices, those who were young in the life – whatever age they might be. And for us, like Christ's mother, their quest was something we constantly pondered in our hearts.

After Christ's parents Mary and Joseph found him in the temple, we are told that 'he went home with them and was obedient to them'. He was nourished and sustained by them in every way, and he grew, as we hoped our Novices would grow, in wisdom and stature. Then came the hidden stage of his journey, those years of living in the holy home of Nazareth. Here, too, there were parallels between the various stages of Christ's life and of our religious life. This growing period for Jesus was the beginning of a journey, a rather silent, low-keyed period, in which the boy needed guidance. Like us, he would have learned of discipline and yet with the flexibility that needed to go with it, so that he too could 'go in and out and find pasture'. One had sometimes found with religious that they fell into three groups. There were those who were black and white and to whom discipline meant a great deal, who dotted every 'i' and crossed every 't', giving no space for manoeuvre, or sometimes even kindness. Then there were those who were too flexible, throwing the necessary disciplines to the wind in order to satiate their own feelings, and who often needed to feel needed. Hopefully, SOLI would only profess those who with a balanced mixture of both had found some measure of wholeness.

By returning to Nazareth and placing himself under the care of his parents, Jesus strengthened the obedience of his heart, learning of work, family life and many other basic, loving values, all of which were wound into his spirituality. This returning to base for a large slice of his life, before starting off along his destined, seemingly more important road of ministry, was reckoned by some to be dull and arduous. Why not just launch forward and get on with it in one's own way? Yet it was as essential for Our Lord as for any called to the spiritual life, and certainly to the religious life, to return to basics to find his true simplicity, in God. Therefore, I reiterate that as Sisters we needed to be able to spiral back to our source, in order to 'become' the people God meant us to be. Thus equipped to do his will we could then travel simply, on a different, more spiritual level.

As said, in Sister Mary Aidan's first paper for Aspirants and Novices came the question: 'Are you willing to enter into a different kind of life, which will change your way of doing things?' In other words, are you ready to begin to mature spiritually, as Jesus matured in his holy home? She also stated that middle-aged people, taking on a new way of life and being, would invariably find it more difficult to make the necessary adjustments. Even so, when the life was embraced in its totality as an act of love for God all things became possible; and positively, all those of us who were committed in our calling could vouch for the wholeness and joy of a true vocation.

Many felt that whatever lifestyle they were living, they had to climb some kind of hierarchical ladder. Here at SOLI there was none of that, although as human beings living in a world where no one was perfect we did, structurally, need to have some framework of authority. Nevertheless, our leadership was a simple, loving one without rancour. A Sister once said to me, when I was feeling particularly responsible with regard to a person whose vocation was not blossoming. 'Mother, no one is responsible for another person.' Up to a point she was right, though what I later discovered was that, as with any parent, one had the responsibility of authority. When authority was vested in anyone in an official capacity, whatever the capacity was, that person undertook the duty of making a good job of his or her office. Hence, our exhortation to incomers was to try and trust those in whose loving care they had been placed, those persons who by the grace of God had been called to such privileged accountability.

The bell at the bottom of the stairs jangled me into thoughts of coffee. So, offering to God all those whom he might send to be future Sisters and Companions of SOLI, I rose and, turning to stoop under the eaves, I too manoeuvred myself down the stairs, for the structure was tight-fitting, to say the least!

Back in the sitting room Sister handed me a mug and sat down with hers. 'Now,' she said, 'tell me about your time away. I don't expect you got around to designing that logo I suggested?'

'No, you're wrong there,' I smiled, 'for actually I did, and it was all a bit unusual. But let me start at the beginning . . .'

My holiday with David and Joan, in North Yorkshire had unexpectedly as it turned out, been strongly linked with my next ports of call and now, looking at the whole time away, it seemed in retrospect preordained. Sister already knew that I had taken the laptop with me, in order to work and maybe to look again at the Rule. What she did not know were any of the details of my trip to Mount Grace. We were both fully aware, however, that it was one of the best-preserved Carthusian charterhouses in England, founded before the Reformation, and that, interestingly, unlike other religious, who lived in common, the Carthusians lived as hermits.

Excitedly, I related this part of my holiday to Sister, describing the small, ruined monastic house, set so beautifully in its tree-clad Yorkshire dale, and of how I had first seen the tower of the church sticking up through the treetops as we had approached. On arriving and stepping into the open cloister, around which were set some vestiges of the monks' cells, I had moved into the sanctuary area between the levelled-off walls of the church. There, I had felt an incredible peace and, at-oneness 'and suddenly,' I told her, 'everything seemed to fall into shape.' That unformed, spindly babe, symbolizing the beginning of our life under a Rule, had not only blossomed into a beautiful child who could stammer a few words, but into one who could now talk and reason and walk, and almost run. And, who knew, maybe one day would take wings and fly!

The next part of my saga caused Sister the greatest astonishment, and despite the fact that it was certainly the most important and culminating part of my time away it was, as I told her, as yet too precious to share with the world and too long to write into this book – in fact it would make a volume in itself. All I could relate of it, in the general sense, was that I met a person chosen of God. In her simplicity, I touched the kind of reality which comes only through the simple and pure of heart, Our Lady herself being the most perfect example. As a result of this remarkable meeting, I also touched something of the reality of Christ and his mother in a new way, one which confirmed many things to me. Most of the time we 'see through a glass darkly', yet just sometimes we are, by pure gift, enabled, through a slit, to see flickers of God's guiding light. In that encounter a door opened and I found something of great value. Mary and Joseph must have felt the same when they found their lost boy, who was such a mixture of youth, vulnerablilty, loving obedience and amazing wisdom. On finding Jesus, his parents must also have seen everything in a new way. Mary certainly pondered it all in her heart . . .

On the day of my encounter, I too found Our Lord in deep simplicity. So often, we humans make life unnecessarily complicated. We make truth such a complex thing, that while we waste time scratching our heads and beating our brains looking for answers, we somehow miss the point. I too had found and had been touched by Christ, the source of all reality, and being obedient to what was asked, found something of Mary and Joseph's own joy. For me, there was now, and I am certain always will be, a wonder about the ordinary, which infiltrated my relationship with God and the whole company of heaven. 'You see,' I explained to Sister Mary Aidan, 'they laugh and care, are wise, and above all they really love.'

'Mother, thank you for sharing that with me,' Sister said. 'I understand now why it can't, as yet, be told publicly. However, there's one thing you've forgotten. You didn't tell me about that other little garden.'

'Oh yes, well, that's easily done. It was like this: on the feast of the Holy Guardian Angels I found myself sitting in a tiny garden. I'd asked my hostess, an elderly lady, if she'd allow me to say Vespers in her summerhouse. There was a carpet on the floor, a chair and a small table inside, and on one of the walls there was a cross. The garden was totally private and, like the hermitage garden at Mount Grace, was backed by woodland. Enchanted by the whole scene of trees in their autumn foliage (for it is always surprising to see trees after the bare landscape of Shetland) I gazed through the doorway, watching two squirrels scuffling around among the leaves. One scurried up a tree trunk and scampered across a branch and then down again and over the rockery. The other rocketed after it. At that hour the sun was high and bright, intensifying the colour of the garden, particularly the flowers, and there was birdsong and, again, great peace. It seemed as though the angels recited the Office with me, sharing the joy. However, the most wonderful thing was – and you'd hardly believe it – the place exuded the same feeling that I'd experienced in the garden of the monk's cell at Mount Grace. It was a personal confirmation of something vitally important. Something that one could only touch fleetingly, and which, like cool fresh water, ran through my hands. Later, as you now know, I was to perceive more.'

'And, finally', said Sister, 'where does the logo fit in?'

I laughed. 'Apropos of all I've told you, the next day held some amazing occurrences, not least that of finding myself in Walsingham. Having visited the place once before I'd never thought to do so again, though I have to acknowledge that what lies beneath its crust is the earliest, probably the most important shrine dedicated to Our Lady in Britain.'

'You enjoyed visiting the shrine church, I'm sure,' Sister said.

'Actually, there was another chapel there that I liked better. I'd seen it from the outside, and its shape, so like ours on Fetlar, had appealed to me. A friend was with me, and although we were short of time, feeling the urge to go inside I pushed open its door. Immediately, we were dazzled by sunshine streaming in through one of two slit windows. The brilliant shaft highlighted the Blessed Sacrament placed in the centre of the altar, causing me to catch my breath, and the smallness and simplicity of the chapel made me feel instantly at home. Then, quite out of character, I found myself walking up to the communion rail in front of the altar and kneeling down. Time stopped, and when it resumed I noticed that the narrow window on my left depicted a modern stained glass design of a spiral! The sun, shining through the heart of it, illuminated the Sacrament . . . Instantly I knew what SOLI's logo should be!'

The Sorrows of Love

7

Love's Sorrows

Lichen grew over the fallen boulders of the disintegrated building thought to have been an old planti-cru of probably a century or two ago. Certainly the crofter and his dependents would have long since gone. Even so, one could still sense a waft of his presence . . . Breathless, having climbed the hill, I flopped on to a sharp rise of ground, a kind of mini broch from where I could survey the isle. A few wisps of mist spiralled around its fringes. Maybe the breeze would blow them out over the ocean or the sun would burn them off. SOLI lay stretched along the southern shoreline and I gazed at it now with its backcloth of blue. A gust of wind puffed an unexpected whiff of peat smoke into my face. Someone must have lit a fire. Glancing along the rooftops on the western side of the hill, I saw the twist of smoke curling upwards from the chimney of a croft house; of course, most of the huddle of houses were now oil-heated or all-electric. Drawing in a breath, I sniffed again, but the elusive scent had disappeared as quickly as it had come.

Goodness, it was difficult to remember when I had last taken time to walk to the top of this bare, moorland brae. Known locally as Halliaria Kirk, it was one of almost a dozen ancient church sites on Fetlar, though this particular location was surrounded by earth mounds. Stretching a leg into a more comfortable position I had to admit that, despite the loveliness of the day, the place had about it a brooding sense of mystery. In earlier years, I had used the spot to draw nearer to God, or to clear my head when making decisions. Others, too, had come here to be alone, including Sister Mary Clare. Actually, during one of her early visits to Fetlar she had come back from the hill, distraught, only saying that she had never been so challenged. Later, I was to learn that she had waged a great battle on this knob as to whether she would join me or not. In her agonizing she had, in the end, said her 'Yes'. For myself, I had never found the hill so unquiet – indeed, had used it on my first visit to confirm an already-made vow to return to Fetlar. Though, when all was said and done, in whatever way one was affected by the place, both Sister and I had found something positive there, something which had stimulated us into action for God.

Closing my eyes I allowed my imagination to run riot. Out through the mists of time came processions of people from every corner of the isle, each making his or her way towards me. On and on they came, filing through the centuries before disappearing into the bogs and dells of a now sparsely populated Fetlar. From annals past they wound, from their brochs and chambered cairns, from the stone circle, from their hermitages and monastic settlements. The Picts lumbered up the slopes from circular, cell-like houses scattered over the isle, appearing as if rising out of the soil. Then came the Finns from Funzie, south east, followed by the missionary Columban-Celtic priests from the crescent-shaped bay of Tresta, in the westerly direction. Through the ages they came; the longboats grating up the beach at Gruting, due east, spilling out Viking warriors who likely settled up the valley that stretched from east to south, and who perhaps later, becoming Christianized, built their Norse monastic settlement over at Strandibrough on the north-eastern point. Or could the Strandibrough site instead have belonged to the Benedictines or Augustinians, who were founding monasteries as far north as Iceland and Greenland at that time? Whatever, all of them traipsed onwards and upwards, until in the sixteenth century the Scottish settlers arrived, increasing the population for a couple more hundred years. Now, they bulged into a great crowd surrounding Halliaria Kirk, in their hand-spun, hand-knitted and woven clothes, carrying their kishies and smiling, before dis-appearing with the others, back, back to what was or was to come, back to their crofts, their ploughs, their boats, back to their place in history – or was it forward into eternity? It was hard to believe that there had been as many as eight hundred people living on Fetlar in those days. Then, alas, the nineteenth century had brought the clearances, when people, pitilessly, were replaced by sheep, and in their devastation the crofters had complained that sheep 'doth eat up men'. Now with those same sheep munching around me I looked out over an isle where the populace had continued to dwindle to fewer than a hundred folk, for many had left to look for work.

My own comparatively short span on Fetlar had begun, gently, with the arrival of the two kittens, Skerry and Flugga. Together we had breathed new life into The Ness, at the foot of the hill. Yet for us, too, time had zoomed forward, taking its course. Skerry had died in his thirteenth year, and now Flugga, at almost eighteen, was also beginning to fail, forcing me to prepare for a second sad farewell.

Lifting the binoculars to my eyes, I looked down at The Ness and saw Sister Mary Cuthbert, a tiny dot in the garden. I smiled, for following in my own tradition she was carving out a new plot from the unyielding land. Barrowing boulders and stones and banging in a stack of elderly fence posts, she worked with zeal. Later, she would cultivate the ground, sow the seed and nourish the plants into growth. In the future, I supposed that in all probability our younger Sister would nourish souls into growth. Having passed through the novitiate, she was now almost through her period of Simple Vows: vows which delightfully set her free, as they had for so many of God's religious before her; vows which could shape a life, if one allowed them to do so, assisting the soul to blossom into spiritual maturity. Conversely, when a vocation was not true the vows imprisoned rather than set free. Anyway, in the not too distant future Sister Mary Cuthbert would be coming up for her election to Life Vows and we were all quietly excited.

Rosemary and I had dropped into the habit of saying the Angelus when up at Halliaria Kirk, so shutting my eyes and in the company of a few gulls, I recited the prayer out loud, ending with the hope, that we would:

'. . . by his passion and cross, be brought to the glory of his resurrection. Amen.'

Truly, life raced on, in the shadow of the passion and cross of Christ. From time immemorial joy had been shot with pain . . . Here, at Halliaria Kirk, all the interwoven, tangled-up dramas of people from the past seemed written into the stones, into the waving tufts of grass, even into the clouds, rain and sun, for all those folk I had envisaged had also pondered, wept and laughed as we do. Yes, we were all a part of that same continuing story of joy and sorrow . . .

Aware of the dampness penetrating my clothing I eased myself up and, slithering down the mound, walked a few steps to the rubble of walls. Was the ruin, in this strange, unexpected location, only a planti-cru? Such structures were usually circular and this was rectangular in shape! Touching the stones I wished that I could have seen the original church or chapel building that had risen from somewhere on this same brow.

Peering around and squeezing my eyes in an attempt to see better in the easterly direction, I located Strandibrough again. Suddenly I wondered if a priest-monk, from that bare promontory where long ago had lain a monastery, could have been connected to or even maybe looked after Halliaria Kirk. Without our modern forms of communication, it would have been possible and even useful perhaps, from such a site as this, to signal his brethren. Was this the reason, then, for a small religious edifice to have been built here? Now I really was imagining things . . . Anyway, even if right, I expected that such a person, from that age, would have been appalled to see a woman priest-religious standing, now, on 'his' sacred ground.

The dedication of the church had always seemed to us a strange one, and as I started off down the track I wondered if it had been named for one of the St Hilarys or perhaps for St Hilarion. Whatever the answer, the building, and as likely as not it had been a small one, would have stood a proud, hilltop beacon. When sitting at my desk in Lark's Hame I had often conjured up the edifice and woven many imaginings around it.

The path home was gentle to start with, and tucking my hands into my wide-sleeved habit I thanked God for so great a plethora of blessings. There had been no monasteries in these isles since the Reformation, and now, down the hill on the sea banks, God had formed SOLI. I remembered how on a certain occasion Rosemary had stood on this same slope with me, looking over the lie of the land spread around us, especially the brochs, and had wondered if such places were built on ley-lines. Later I learned that ley-lines were a comparatively recent invention, and when mentioning this to an archaeologist friend recently was not surprised to find that her response was one of silent amusement!

Albeit, whatever mysteries were embedded in these rocks, I felt as though SOLI had become an integral part of them, part of this small corner of the earth, part of that great winding pageant, and part of a long spiritual line established here for a particular reason. Like the mustard seed spoken of by Christ, we were a small grain cast into the earth, and only time would tell . . .

Skidding down an unexpected dip, I found that the field was becoming increasingly soggy. What a good thing that I had put my gumboots on. Holding on to the fence along the now indistinguishable path, I turned again to look up to the ancient site, and I found that the mist had enveloped it entirely while, down below, Aithness was snatched into a pool of sunlight. Suddenly, out of the blue, another fence, strung with broken bits of barbed-wire, loomed ahead, and wriggling under it as carefully as possible so as not to tear my habit, I jagged a finger on an uncompromising barb. 'Blow and ouch!' I hissed, unwinding myself from an undignified position and at the same time trampling my cord into a puddle. Sighing, for the bottom of my habit was now splattered with mud, I straightened up. Then, dashing the blood from my hand and sucking my finger, I glanced once more up the hill. Christ's crucifixion had been on the brow of a hill, I reflected, and after his arduous ascent with the cross on his back, he had been murdered that we might live. This, if anything, was reason enough for us, SOLI, to make our sharing of his Passion, his agony and scourging, a positive part of our own journey into wholeness – whatever our stumbling. The brow had again disappeared, and looking down at my punctured finger, I thought of the crown of thorns pressed into the head of Our Lord.

Wrapping a handkerchief around the gash, I hooked the skirt of my habit around my waist before paddling through more bog. Yes, pain, I conjectured, came in many ways and was all part of that skein of sorrow which threaded itself in and out of our lives. Yet there was also joy . . . and who knew, perhaps the two, woven

together, would make, at the last, the garment of glory? Whatever the case, it was clear that for anyone called to the Christian
life, whether they were a religious or not, either of these attrib-
utes of joy or sorrow could be the more prevalent at a given time,
and somehow I could not help feeling that always, between the
two, hung that 'perfect balance'.

On the whole, joy permeated SOLI's offering – certainly it was
so for me. Within the community, we had each been asked to risk
the giving of all, and in great vulnerability had opened ourselves to
pain and darkness in a way that took courage. But, in the receiving
of our offerings, God had both protected and blessed us with joy.
Accordingly, in our standing unprotected before him and in our
submission to his will, we found ever deepening fulfilment. This
did not exonerate us from the occasional grumbling about our
difficulties, or from a wild, out-of-sync personal aspiration or two,
for we were still human; nevertheless, our offerings had been
made, and we knew that the way forward, be it clothed in joy or
sorrow, was of God's choosing and not our own, and that whatever was asked of us, his will was the only perfect way. One happy
thing, for sure, was that if our lives were truly offered to and in
Love, nothing could be lost. In my own experience, over the years
God had more and more given himself to us, out of all proportion
to our giving to him. This did not mean that sorrow evaporated
but, on the contrary, that the shadowy, painful side of our lives
enabled new spiritual growth. No one could escape pain, especially
Love's pain. That was the reason why, when we were asked why
God allowed this or that to happen to us, one could only answer
that it was simply a fact of the world, and that no one was exempt
from suffering. Remarkably, God had not even allowed himself
that pleasure, for sorrow was an integral part of redemption.

Over Sister Mary Clare's departure to Orkney, I had known
sorrow. Indeed, as said, no one was exempt . . . For us at SOLI, we
knew that new vocations would come and go and relatively few

would stay. We were also aware that those who tested their vocation here would need, in some degree, to follow Christ's way of the cross. First would come those 'agonies' of doubt about their vocation, then the 'scourging' of growing into a new life. Later, the 'thorny crown' of the vows would be placed on their head, and finally, death itself would bring this life's only release.

Walking on I continued to think of Sister Mary Clare. She was the first to join me, apart from Rosemary and those two scamps Skerry and Flugga, and her absence had left a gap. Yet, again, we were all different, and individual choices had to be made. Perhaps it was not so surprising after all, when life's pattern was made up of such varied shapes.

Climbing the last fence, I smoothed out my habit and stepped out on to our road to Aithness. Thinking of shapes, the shape of my habit was not looking too good . . . Had I seen another Sister so dishevelled I would have raised my eyebrows! In the community to which I had belonged in Devon, we had been taught – and rightly so – that our habit was the outward sign to ourselves and to the world of an interior life, given wholly and completely to God in desire and will; indeed, woe betide any of us who had not taken pains to keep it in good order. There, too, I learned that within the state of holy poverty, it did not matter how patched or mended one's garments were: indeed, that it was honourable to wear such attire for God. And also, when dressing and undressing we were exhorted to call to mind the prayers said over our habit on our clothing and profession days, so that the habit might become a continual reminder to us of the purpose of our life in the state of holy religion. We each had a prayer of St Francis pinned to the crucifix in our cell, a prayer which we were to say when dressing each morning:

Ah Lord! With thy pierced hands, do thou clothe me with the raiment of charity, that my soul appear not naked in thy sight.

SOLI's religious habit was cut in the shape of the cross, Christ's own symbol to the world, signifying redemption. The cord represented the scourge with which he was flogged, and the three knots in our cord served as a constant reminder to us of the three vows we had made. Our sandals were the sign of a pilgrim, and the veil tied around our heads covered our hair, which in ages past was said to be a woman's crowning glory. The reason for the veil had been to signify that a female was no longer on the marriage market. In our case it was the sign of our being given wholly to Christ. So each part of the attire had a meaning, and not only was it there to help us to fulfil our particular vocation, but also to make each of us, whoever we were, equal. We all looked the same and so there was no room for glamour or to keep up with the fashions or buy expensive garments. In reality, the habit brought a release and freedom from worldly vanity and belongings. Our particular habit or tunic was simple and easily thrown over our heads. Some religious communities, following much more modern trends, had relaxed considerably their rule of wearing a habit, though my great fear for anyone doing so was that it might prove to be the thin end of the wedge. Of course, we were fully aware that wearing a religious dress did not necessarily make us better Sisters. What we did know though, was that if we truly gave something up for God, be it the right to choose what we wore or anything else, he returned it a hundredfold, and it was often as though we had given nothing at all – St Paul was so right when he said, 'as having nothing and yet possessing everything'.[1]

So, the habit was a small part of our witness to God and to the world, of a group of people given entirely to God in will and in heart, a group of people who witnessed to living in Christ's love and in their unity became a family in God. 'And all who were together were of one heart and mind.'

A lot of people had said – and who were we to say otherwise? – that the world was better able to relate to monks and nuns if they wore lay clothing, yet somehow I felt the world had grown used to the monastic garb over centuries and perhaps understood more of its significance than we gave it credit for. Anyway, I had a feeling that if secular fashions suddenly changed to that of wearing a habit-type garment, many people would wear it and think it 'cool'. In fact, in the climate of our present day, perhaps we needed a few more obvious symbols of religion. It did not say much about the spiritual life of a monk or nun if they were not obvious, though of course it had to be said that if Christ himself shone through them then, whatever they wore, they would be sought out by those who would delight in their company.

As I trundled down our narrow road I saw something that made me stop in my tracks: it looked like an otter sidling up the grass verge. Proceeding quietly and more cautiously I drew nearer, only to discover with mingled disappointment and pleasure that it was Mooskit. Looking up, he saw me and sauntered in my direction, and despite his apparent disdain, he sniffed the mud around the hem of my habit and accompanied me home.

8

Love's Way

Sister Mary Cuthbert had been wondering if we might introduce a few hens to the plot at the back of The Ness. We all thought this a lovely idea, though realized that we would need to build some kind of a poultry house first. A little undecided, Sister left the whole question in soak throughout the summer, concentrating her energies, instead, into the growing of vegetables. Actually, Jean had taken into her charge (along with Iona the goat) a hen given to her by a local crofter. Over the colder months, having answered to many cluckings and then tappings on her door, she had become fond of the bird. How could she, and later Rose (for Lower Ness was nearby), not treat 'Hen', as she was called, to a few pecks of food and an odd meal, and then to a daily meal and afterwards to a fair amount of care, in return for a few eggs?

'Hen'

I could not help feeling sorry for those religious communities whose rule forbade the keeping of creatures. Such institutions would have good reason for the 'no animals' regulation, and this we respected, though at the same time I cherished the fact that our roots, coming from Franciscanism, blessed us with the privilege of sharing our life with a few of God's furry and feathered ones. Christ's love had obviously encompassed them all when on earth, for he had used them as examples when teaching. It seemed probable – and delightful, too – that he had been born in the midst of them, in the stable. Later, there was the ass which carried him into Jerusalem on Palm Sunday and the cock that crowed on Good Friday and, of course, all the other references to the birds of the air, the fish in the sea and the sheep of the pasture. Anyway, whatever anyone said, we loved our menagerie of two dogs, a goat, a hen, the two cats over at St Mahri's Hame and, now sadly alone, only one puss, in the form of Mooskit, at Aithness.

Flugga was only a small, and towards the end of his life, frail little cat, yet for me, he and his brother Skerry had held a huge place at the heart of our lives, especially since they were the first two members of SOLI to arrive at Aithness. The memory of a couple of tiny kittens hurling themselves in mock battle up and down the stairs at The Ness was as clear a picture now as if it was yesterday. Flugga, totally different in temperament though as equally dear as his twin, became a beloved companion to all of us. Nevertheless, he could be as naughty as the next, especially when targeting unsuspecting guests, who were always his easiest pushovers! With astounding persistence he had a unique way of demanding the attention of any spare human possessing a potentially spare lap, and none could thwart him! Sitting on Sybil's writing pad was a favourite ploy, one especially designed to wheedle her into the utility room to dole out yet another helping of cat food. In fact, during his last six years of living at Lark's

Flugga

Hame, he played Sybil and me off against each other appallingly, and became thoroughly spoiled. In short, he had us both tightly wrapped around his four little paws, especially with regard to tummy matters!

Latterly, of course, we all knew that Flugga was living on borrowed time. Our vet gave him only a few weeks to live many months before his actual demise, but he was a plucky fellow – and, as one was only too aware, animals did not spend as much of their lives dwelling upon themselves as we humans, who (to quote my Reverend Mother of long ago) 'are always thinking about how we feel and where we feel it now'!

Alas, though, the final moment came, and with sinking heart I drove our little friend his last 50 miles, plus the two ferry crossings, over to our vet on the Shetland Mainland. Flugga never made a fuss when travelling by car, and on this occasion curled up and slept silently beside me. Every moment was special, and how I grudged the solicitude which would not allow me to waken him.

Covering the 18 miles over the island of Yell, about the only car on the road that morning, I drove directly into the rising sun. It stretched blood-red fingers between bare hills and drew my thoughts, as always, towards the incredible reality of God – towards the magnitude of his love, and towards the wonder which will be revealed to us at our own transition from darkness into light, from death into life. Nevertheless, we all 'ken' as they say up here, that despite any human glimpses through the sometimes so 'thin veil', we could none of us escape the fact that we were still en route through a burdensome, earthly span of life; and this being so, such glorious certainties of the beyond were tinged, for me on that day, with the gloom of sadness! This, of course, should not have been such a surprising truth, knowing as we did that our souls, imprisoned in the chrysalis of their own mortality, were still toiling towards the throwing off of our constantly dying physical bodies. However, onwards we strained, sometimes painfully, yet always, thank God, towards that ultimate bursting forth . . . towards that new beginning, at the so-called 'end of our lives' . . . towards our new birth into Christ, into the eternal, into the dawn of the soul's hard-won freedom from life into life.

We rumbled on to the next ferry and Flugga opened his eyes. I stroked his head and heard the tiniest of purrs.

Truly, the passing out of our sight of loved ones, albeit into light, whether they be human or animal, left most of us who had known love tossing violently between the certainty of God's eternity and our own emotional, earthly feelings of death's finality – of its separation and pain. Clearly, we could not help such feelings of bereavement, nor perhaps should, for somehow it seemed as though our sufferings shuffled us forward through the density of this temporary lodging, where we saw only 'through a glass darkly . . .'

Lyndsay, the vet, was waiting for us when we arrived, and so was Sister Mary Aidan, St Mahri's Hame being only a few miles from the veterinary practice. Having examined Flugga thoroughly and explored every avenue, which included taking a blood test, Lyndsay was adamant that it would not be kind to keep him alive. All hope vanished! Then she, whose vocation was one of normally preventing death, moved into the gentle coaxing of this our precious friend towards the entry into his own new day. Sister Mary Aidan and I were deeply moved. So it happened that Flugga's quiet passing from death into life, into the 'cat life' of heaven, into that most holy place which would one day receive us all, was complete.

How wonderful God was, I thought, as I drove home. Beside me was the tissue-lined shoebox which Sybil had helped me prepare the night before in case our uneasy premonitions were right. Tears dampened my face. How dear he was, he who gave us the privilege of sharing our lives with these loving creatures whom we presumed to call our 'lower brethren', those little ones from whom we learned so much about God's own unconditional love for us. Their innocence and trust seemed always so sharp to me, in contrast to the often complaining and whingeing behaviour of people. We of SOLI would certainly be giving great thanks for the gift which Flugga's tiny life had given us.

The road seemed endless that night, and driving home, I conjured up pictures of my mother, long since dead. I imagined her, who had so cared for our own family cat, now welcoming Flugga with great love – for love, of all things could not die. Unsurprisingly, I also became aware of Rosemary, who of course had loved and known Fluggy from kittenhood. Suddenly I got a sharp sense of her speaking, in that adamant way of hers. She seemed to be saying: 'Don't forget that I'm here too . . . here for Flugga and for all of you!'

It was late when I arrived home that night and placed the shoebox containing its furry cargo on a low table in chapel, in front of the altar. I covered it with a white sacristy cloth and it lay there, 'in state' as it were, until after our Sung Mass the next morning, at the end of which we carried the little body up to the rock garden, where Sister Mary Cuthbert had prepared a grave by the side of Skerry's. We buried tiny Flugga, feeling poignantly that his death had symbolically sealed a stretch of our journey along our own way of the cross. Certainly it brought to an end the first era of SOLI – for that particular week commemorated the anniversary of our official recognition as a religious community, some dozen years before. As is our custom when burying a pet, we cut free a raft of balloons, in this instance with Flugga's name written on each one of them, and there, on the edge of the world – our cliff-top home – they caught the breeze and soared skywards.

Unequivocally, the years rolled on . . . and standing by the graveside at the beginning of another new chapter of life we asked Our Lord to bless and bring us all, in his most perfect timing, to the joys of love's ultimate reunion. 'Ashes to ashes and dust to dust', death into life and life into God!

9

Love Sacrificed

Pain gnawed at the usual elation I felt when returning to Shetland. The reflections of sunset, flaring off the sea, rippled around the cabin, tinting everything inside rose-coloured. Unusually, on this occasion its warmth brought no comfort. Yes, love hurt, and any kind of, 'passing on' or 'farewell' we experienced inevitably left in its wake an empty feeling, which could not immediately be filled. Pulling my breviary from my bag I laid it on the bunk at my side. During the 14-hour journey home on the ship I had planned to complete some work, say Vespers and have a bite of supper before bed. Yet my mind would not oblige nor be filled with anything other than the inert ache of bereavement. Our Lady must have felt agonies of numbness when her Son was bundled down from the cross . . . and for her, there must have been a hopeless reaching out to touch something that could no longer be touched, to hear a voice that seemed no longer there, to love and feel no love in return. It was that dull pain known to us all, especially to mothers, in some form or other, and it was a pain which would not go away. Albeit I knew that eventually, however impossible it seemed, it would be lifted, and as Mother Julian so rightly said, that in the end all would be well.

Having journeyed to Aberdeen the night before, I was now returning on the same ship back to the Northern Isles. The reason for my trip was that the first person whom God had sent to join me as a Sister, Sister Mary Clare, had finally decided that she could no longer continue along the path which SOLI trod. Having lived three years away from Shetland, partly to discern her direction, the moment had now come to grasp back her freedom to serve God as she wished, rather than as our Rule dictated. This meant a dispensation from her vows made to God as a Sister. Like the dove that Noah released from the ark I now tried to let go of a spiritual daughter, Sister and friend . . .

As one discovered early in the religious life, pain was like a sharp tool which cut deeply, yet the cavity it carved within could, potentially, become a capacity to be filled with joy. In struggling, over the years, to encourage Sister to 'stay with it', I had finally to accept that, for her, the vows imprisoned rather than brought freedom. We all needed the freedom 'to be', and when it was missing one knew that something was awry. Hence, it was not necessarily negative reasons which caused persons to abandon the religious life. Painfully for a few, however, their leaving was due to such issues as 'the giving up of personal control'. To start with, it was never easy to relinquish one's so-called 'right' of making decisions without that first obtaining of certain permissions. Trusting one's life to God, to the extent of placing it in the fallible hands of other human beings was a daunting request, for nothing was harder than saying to him, 'Thy will be done,' and truly meaning it, at least in the sense of risking all! This setting aside of pride and leaving of all our desires, ambitions, home, family and friends to follow Christ totally was a sacrifice that few understood or were prepared to make. So, instead of the life bringing the security it should, it actually brought much questioning and uncertainty. It was, again, a strange contradictory fact known only to those who had experienced the joy of letting everything go and trusting in some power greater than themselves, that in doing so they became more fully themselves and received a far greater freedom in their service of God. Personally, in the continued giving of myself, which I was aware would take more than this lifetime to learn, I had found, especially over the past two or three years, that one was gifted with a different kind of control, a control called 'total love'. Consequently, when a person genuinely cut loose from self, she or he found a freedom which was of heaven and a knowledge which told them that Love, and Love only, could unbind.

Sister Mary Clare, Bishop Bruce (our Primus and the Episcopalian Bishop of Aberdeen and Orkney who was SOLI's official Visitor) and I had met together that day in the diocesan office in Aberdeen, and Sister had been released from her vows and all obligations to SOLI. It was heart-breaking for us all, and definitely one of the most difficult experiences I had ever had. Afterwards, sitting on a wall overlooking the beach, we had gazed across the North Sea, and while there had had our own private service of blessing:

> O everlasting Father,
> Creator of all things,
> Take this your servant, Mary Clare,
> In your own generous clasp,
> In your own generous arm.
>
> May you be with her in every pass,
> With her on every hill . . .

A Fetlar beach

After two days, back at home and still feeling fragile, I wandered down to the beach of Aithness, where I regained enough equilibrium to write the following letter to our friends:

My dear Caim Members and friends,

Although our little beach is only five minutes away I rather shockingly haven't been there for several summers, at least not to appreciate it at a deep level. This morning Shuna and I changed all of that and spent a couple of hours enjoying the different things that the tiny cove had to offer. She dashed madly around, up and down the banks, over the shingle and splashed back and forth in and out of the sea, only stopping to rub up against me or shake off a shower of wetness; we have recently discovered that she's a real water dog. My pleasure in the beach was not so energetically felt or displayed, you'll be pleased to know! Indeed, bearing in mind that I am nearly twenty years older than when I first arrived in Fetlar, I just opted to sit, only allowing the beauty of the place to stir a few thoughts. Nature, in such places and on such a summer's day, is often spiritually revitalizing, sharpening the senses with a feast of sight, sound and scents. The tide, on the ebb, rolled wavelets over the pebbles, dragging from them a deep chuntering song. Sea birds swooped and dived, and in the warmth of the sun everything glimmered in a way that I had almost forgotten.

Having returned from a fleeting visit to Aberdeen two days ago, I needed to take stock of our life here, and to reflect upon how I would write this most important letter to you.

The reason for my trip to Aberdeen was in order that on behalf of SOLI, I could, with Bishop Bruce, release Sister Mary Clare from her vows and bless her in her new spiritual pilgrimage forward. Her dispensation from the religious vows (made within SOLI's more eremitical calling) had been mutually agreed upon, in order that she might travel along a pathway which will lead her to a place where she is able to embrace a much more active lifestyle, which she hopes will be in the area of working among people with practical needs. The freedom to follow this route is something that she has desired for a long time, and so after a period of discernment for all of us, we now send her forth, with love.

Mary Clare's new journey will almost immediately take her to Romania with a women's Christian organization called the Lydia Project. There, she will be working with groups of women who bring people together from economically devastated societies, creating different ways forward in the way of teaching skills such as English, gardening and needlework, achieving all kinds of practical goals and sharing experiences. After Romania we do not know in which direction God will lead her, though pray that this exciting, if not slightly daunting, road will bring peace, happiness and wholeness of soul. She is thinking at the moment that, ultimately, she will return to live in Orkney – though not as part of the Hamarfiold Trust project that she has helped set up, and the Trustees will of course be taking that venture forward themselves, so perhaps you could pray for them also. Mary Clare has two pensions, but with a legacy, and a sum of money from SOLI to help her get started, she is confident that she can maintain the sort of lifestyle she envisages. She will be reverting to her former name of Mary, though it is likely that SOLI will continue to call her Mary Clare.

The ebbing and flowing of all our lives in this world pulsates in a fairly regular rhythm through good and ill, sunshine or storm, joy or sorrow, synchronizing so many things – the days, the months and the whole cycle of the seasons and years, all of them impossible to hold back. In my ponderings on SOLI's so short span, I looked at those great boulders on the shore, and found it amazing to think that they had remained so immovable through centuries of gale and calm, while at the same time other objects, created in the same order of things, had moved and changed at all manner of copious, evolutionary speeds. We all know, of course, that change is inevitable, whether it be slow or fast, and hopefully that it spells 'growth and wholeness'. Also, as most of us are aware, change, in its truest sense, is all a part of creation's moving forward towards its ultimate perfection, is all a part of God's wonderful creativity in the bringing about of his unique plan. During my own time on this isle things have certainly grown and changed and, I hope, have matured towards greater fullness.

Many things had changed down on the shore, I noticed. The course of the stream falling down the banks had widened; Willie Petrie's old boat has now almost completely disintegrated into the long grasses; the face of the cliff was smoother in places and, if possible, even more smothered with sea pinks. Some more moveable seashore objects had been caught up by the tide, shells and rocks lodged in new crevices, pebbles sifted, shuffled here and there across the beach, and a fishing net and a broken box spewed up over fresh ridges of seaweed. Other things had perhaps, unusually in some cases, been carried off to new lands, certainly cast up on different shorelines by bird or wave. Not surprisingly, then, the beach this morning made me realize afresh how vital change and movement were in the bringing about of God's will. It also helped me to re-acknowledge how everyone, each creature and thing, be they animate or inanimate, is all part of an amazing, gigantic, moving pattern of life that is woven into a web called Christ, a beautiful, glorious garment called Love, created with the strands of pain, of sorrow and joy. Furthermore, I found it comforting to remember that, despite any problems that life might throw at us, the wonderful thing was, that God was the weaver at the loom, and that it was he, ever in charge, who was using everything, not only for the world's eventual benediction and good, but for the good of each one of us, too – each one of us who loved him.

In that same love, we wish you a happy summer,

+Mary Agnes S.O.L.I.

Later, kneeling in chapel before our Office of Vespers began, I thanked God for the gift of love. Despite any of the hurts it had brought, or might bring in the future, love was Love, and ultimately would overcome pain. It was Love who had come into the world, not to condemn it but to save it through his death, and I prayed that in whatever way we were called to follow him, we might do so humbly and with the same obedience.

Rising from her seat, Sybil walked over to the bell-rope and tugged it into life, and the Office of Vespers began with the ringing out of the Angelus . . .

Behold the handmaid of the Lord.
Be it unto me according to thy word . . .
 . . . Holy Mary
  . . . pray for us now and in the hour of our death . . .

Death! Yet death would always bring with it the hope of a glorious resurrection!

The Glories of Love

10

Love Resurrected

Death was always the precursor of resurrection, and my next journey south, less than a couple of months after Mary Clare had flown to Romania, had a hint of glory about it that surprised me. This time, standing with elbows on the sill of a west-facing porthole with my breviary propped against the glass, I said Compline, hardly able to take my eyes from the stream of light flooding across the water. Every kind of red and golden-amber sunset hue glistened and glinted, swirling exotic patterns around the walls, while the ship plunged forward into the night. Suddenly I remembered the seasickness pill that I should have taken an hour before the journey started. Since one never knew exactly how rough or calm the sea would prove to be, or whether there would be a great nauseating swell, it was wise to take precautions. Of course, if the crossing was bad, 14 hours of not being able to disembark was a long time! Groping into a bag, I found the anti-sickness pills and swallowed one. Under the circumstances, it was better to get to bed promptly and lie flat. Undressing, I took a quick shower and then, dropping the bunk down from the cabin wall, pulled a half-written sermon from my luggage. My journey was to England, and I needed to finish preparing for a wedding service at which I would be officiating; the boat, as always, provided a good opportunity. Snuggling under the duvet and propping my head with two pillows, I glanced through the pages.

Scanning the first page, my eyes fastened on my text, which seemed a suitable one, I felt, for the making of marriage vows, or for that matter the making of any form of commitment to God. It told how many waters could not quench love, nor the floods drown it . . . And now as this sea of waters carried me away from my beloved home in Shetland, I contemplated the truth of those scriptural words, that no ocean of waters, however violently overwhelming or furious those waters were, could ever quench love. Ceaselessly, this capstone of truth taught us that in every up and down of life, no matter what, love was immortal and that all would be well, and all tears wiped from our eyes, barring for one reason only – that we, individually, allowed any or all of those outer pressures or turbulent storms of life to quench our love, and so extinguish the eternal essence of who we were.

Yes, I must tell the young couple that under those earthly crusts of ours we were love, and that every one of us was made in the image of love, for Love was God. Somehow, I must also ascertain that when two people were brought together in holy matrimony, they were made one in him, so that two loves became one love, and coming together made so strong a single unit of love that they were able to conceive love in the shape of their children . . . For me, there was nothing more important in the whole world or in our lives than this love; not hope, not joy, not peace or any other thing, for love encapsulated and was the ultimate of all things. Our life was a being called forward in love by Love himself to participate in a journey of love; and for us, as religious, our vows were as binding as any marriage, for ultimately our binding became a binding with Love himself.

In my mind, I longed to share with the young couple and the congregation in church something of this journey of love. In Shetland, of course, there was much journeying, for there were many islands, and in order to travel from one island to another one had to take a boat. On a summer's day this could be idyllic, with glassy waters, puffins, incredible views, reflections and, sometimes, extraordinary sights. One day I was lucky enough to be able to lean over the rails and watch five killer whales hardly a boat-length away. However, up here in the far north it was on the whole either winter or summer, with little spring or autumn between, and as you will imagine, generally the winter was as wild as the summer was calm.

Tonight our crossing south to Aberdeen seemed extraordinarily calm, and lying there I enjoyed the gentle rocking of the bed. Yes, whatever our circumstances, we were all of us without exception on a voyage, or if you liked on a journey through 'earth time'. Metaphorically, we knew that our lives would be affected by outer things, and that in this world there would always be seasonal variations of the elements, including extremes, so that sometimes the journey would be calm and beautiful, sometimes ordinary and at other times dark and terrible. Believing, as I did, that we were part of that continuing cycle which had in reality neither beginning nor end, I knew that there was nothing we could do to change the purpose of God's will. Sliding my notes and a Bible on to the table by the bed I turned off the light. In effect, our earthly journey was like those journeys over the waters of Shetland. It was a selection of amazing trips, which could be an unutterably beautiful, adventurous, terrifying, painful part of our getting to a particular place; all of them a part of our voyage into wholeness, a part of our travelling from, and into, the vast, uncharted dimensions of the eternal.

Certainly, from the day of their wedding, my young couple, in their journeying forward, would not only need to protect, honour and comfort each other but also to trust in the strength of their love. As with all Christian people, they would be going forward into the unknown, yet at the same time into the joy of their pilgrimage, and to some extent they would require to do this in company. Also, they needed to know that those joys would of necessity be interwoven with sorrow, which could be scary. Yet finally, at the end and through the doorway of death, would come glory! Death would be transformed in life, into resurrection, and drawn into that cusp where the end became the beginning, the ebbing of the tide became the flowing, and the waning of life its waxing.

The glory of the Resurrection of Christ stayed with me that night, weaving in and out of my mind with thoughts for the wedding homily, and not surprisingly I awoke the next morning to words that could have been of the resurrected one himself: 'Rise up, my love, and come.' Yes, 'Come, all of you,' he seemed to be saying, 'come travel together with me, travel to me, travel to my awaiting glory.'

Throwing off the duvet and rubbing my eyes I eased up and looked through the window. Aberdeen was in sight, with the sun glinting across its rooftops. Another new day had dawned . . . As always, night had merged with day, as our journeying on earth merged with our journeying in heaven – of which, I repeat, our minds, bodies and souls were all part of that pulsating cycle, that spiral which at its optimum ascended upwards towards where Christ, risen and glorified, was the summit of all our strivings. In truth, he who was our God constantly called us forward into a deeper life . . . Getting up, I prayed that we might all journey courageously together, in the strength and joy of his love.

A few days later, with happy memories of the wedding, I found myself once more in North Yorkshire. Having planned a concentrated week with my computer, my aim was to start this book before returning home. David and Joan, respecting my needs, again gave me space in their lovely stone flat above the garage.

The morning of brilliant September sunshine was warm by Shetland standards; so, with the temperatures hotter than a midsummer's day in the north and with a notebook and pen in my pocket, I wandered around the garden before starting work, finding, once more, that the grounds were full of unexpected vistas and crannies. There was a partially hidden summerhouse in one direction, facing across fields and layers of blue-grey forestry, and over the boundary fence sheep grazed, oblivious of this world's troubles. Central to the garden was laid out a curvaceous lawn, overhung with giant deciduous trees and splayed with herbaceous shrubs and plants. Sunlight stippled the grass and a warm breeze shook a desultory leaf or two across an already leaf-strewn tapestry of colour. The remaining foliage murmured in the breeze, merging its rustlings and creaking of branches into a concerto of country sounds. I stared upwards, delighting in the dashes of blue sky through the treetops. Wood pigeons cooed and the sheep, stimulated into sudden thoughts of extra food, greeted a farm truck on the forestry track with a cacophony of noise. Unlatching a gate, its wood warm to the touch, and winding through a shrubbery I came upon a delightfully sub rosa secret nook. Draped in greenery it was cool and hidden. Brushing a few leaves from a wrought-iron seat, which had an accompanying table, I sat for a while and, enjoying the new scents and sounds, watched a robin and his mate flutter in and out of the bushes and over a pond. A gravel path led to an almost life-size statue of St Francis feeding the birds, where trailers of roses and escallonia reached tendrils towards him, twining over a metal arch and spiralling about his skirts. Overhead, the almost cloudless sky could be seen, this time through a latticework of leaves, branches, rose hips and rowan berries. I breathed my thanks to God for human life on such a day.

Had that other garden of long ago, where the grief-stricken St Mary Magdalene saw her beloved Christ, been so lovely, I asked. And how was it that neither she nor his disciples had at first recognized so close a friend? Were we, too, as dull of hearing and seeing? He had appeared so humbly; as a gardener to Mary, as a wayfarer to the Emmaus disciples, and of course, from the beach, a seeming stranger, he had watched the disciples in their boat on the water. Interestingly, only John had called out from the lake that it was the Lord! Gradually, of course, they were all enlightened. Fiery tongues were later to set their hearts ablaze . . . and Christ to open their minds as, hopefully, he would open ours . . .

Mary Magdalene had understood almost instantly when he spoke her name . . . I listened now, knowing that he spoke mine – along with all the names of those I loved, both in this world and in the next.

After a while, moving back to the rambling house, I wandered along a pathway which led around a conservatory and into the full sunlight of an orchard of dwarf apple trees. Set among them there was another metal table, this time with four matching chairs. Sitting on one of them I pulled a notebook from my pocket with the intention of work, though soon, feeling comatose and very lazy in the warmth of the sun, leant back and closed my eyes. At that moment, David appeared with a tray of drinks. 'Come along, Mother, and have coffee in the garden-room,' he called.

The garden-room was a nearby stone building with glass doors along the whole of one side. These had been opened to the sun, reminding me in an exaggerated way of the tomb of the Resurrection. Joan, whose turn it was to lead her church's inter-cessions the following Sunday, was ensconced already, seated in a basket chair and, like me, scratching away in a notebook. She, too, was pleased to be interrupted. Afterwards, I returned to the orchard, this time to work in earnest. Even so, I could not help gazing around for just a moment, wondering how often Rose-mary had also sat there and of what she had been thinking.

Where there was love, I began to write, neither death nor any other thing could separate us from it, or from those whom we had and still loved. Folk often suggested that we must miss Rosemary a lot since she died but, wonderfully, we knew that she was still with us, in a totally new way, though to our minds equally in heaven! The world with all its machinations could not obliterate what truly was, only that which was not. Here, in David and Joan's garden, a garden which Rosemary knew so well, her presence was almost as tangible as it so often seemed in our chapel, at home.

Yes, I thought, gradually the disciples had become aware of Christ's presence, yet in their case in an incredible and indescribable way . . . they had touched his glory and been ignited by it, and he had exhorted them to pass his gift on to the world. We too had received that same privilege of showing forth his glory to the world in whatever way he asked. Admittedly, there were dimensions around us to which our senses were often dulled; even so, the veil was thin and one day we too would see and hear and, understanding, share the full wonder of the God who died and rose again. Then, perhaps it would be for us as Isaiah had prophesied:

For as the earth puts forth her blossom or the bushes in the garden burst into flower, so shall the Lord God make righteousness and praise blossom before all nations.[1]

11

Love Lifted High

For one reason or another, including illness, Sister Mary Aidan's annual holiday had twice been postponed, and this year we had agreed that nothing should prevent it happening. Like me, her reluctance to take a break was not so much that of not wishing to visit her friends, but rather that she loved her life in Shetland and was of the age when it seemed a lot of effort and energy to pack and travel. Anyway, plans were made, and given that I was the only person who could be spared from Fetlar to house-and-cat-sit while she was away, I had arrived at St Mahri's Hame, laden with a laptop, printer and files.

Since returning from Yorkshire a month earlier, there had been several priorities which kept me from my desk and now I had only one end in sight – that of settling back into our winter routine, and getting on with this book. Deadlines were apt to creep up unawares, as every author will know, and since the volume was of importance to SOLI, I had already begun to feel panicky. It was at that point that Sister had made her suggestion. 'Mother,' she proffered, 'why don't you come and cat-sit, yourself? Sister Mary Cuthbert could look after things at home, and honestly, you wouldn't need to worry about a thing over here . . . Excepting, of course, to care for the cats and get on with the book. No one would bother you, and knowing Wilma, she'd probably pop up with the odd stew!' After much consideration, for I had spent more time away from home over those recent months than I had ever done, I decided that it was an opportunity to be taken. So one Sunday morning, after the Sung Eucharist on Fetlar, I set off to the west side, and on my arrival found Sister in the midst of her packing. 'Do put your things in my office, Mother,' she called out, 'and I'll be with you in a moment.'

In no time at all, I was on my knees grappling with cables and setting the scene for a fortnight's tapping away. 'You know where the power points are, don't you, Mother?' Sister checked. 'And I'll give you an extra table if you like . . . ?' Having looked in to see how I was progressing, she was conveniently handy to answer the telephone when it rang. Strangely, it was one of those occasions when I felt that the call might just be for me, so, pausing, I waited to be passed the receiver. The caller turned out to be a Fetlar friend, Aileen, asking if I would attend a funeral on the island of Yell. 'It's in two days, and could you give the tribute?' she invited. Innocently oblivious of my proposed timetable, she explained that the service was for a relative of hers who had died the week before. Since the deceased had been a good friend of mine, I agreed – though not without some alarm!

Dorothy had taught me most of what I knew about writing, and not a little, I might add, of what I knew about cats, for she also had been a doting owner. The tribute would need serious thought. Ah well, I reckoned, sidelining the manuscript for another day ought not to make too much difference.

As things turned out, my being on the Shetland Mainland proved more useful than we anticipated, for not only was I able, the next morning, to drive Sister Mary Aidan to the airport but also to arrange a meeting with our bishop, who having made a flying visit to Shetland was returning to Aberdeen on the same flight as Sister. The Reverend Martin Oxley, our Warden and Rector of St Magnus, Lerwick, also joined us, and after some constructive dialogue, Martin and I waved the travellers off. That same day, Sybil was admitted to hospital in Lerwick for a second cataract operation – which was opportunely arranged, since after her surgery I was on hand to transport her to Yell. There at the ferry terminal we met Rose, who continued the journey to Fetlar.

Returning to St Mahri's Hame, and true to Sister's word, Wilma called in, to deposit all kinds of goodies she thought would make life easier. After she left, I fed Barney and Pippin, said Vespers and settled myself at Sister's desk, wondering what I could say in tribute to Dorothy.

Almost twenty years before, I had stood at the reception desk of the P&O ferry terminal in Aberdeen waiting to be handed two boarding cards. Suddenly, to my surprise I felt a firm grip on my shoulder from behind, and swinging around found a gentleman standing there. 'Excuse me, Sister, are you the nun who's coming to live on Fetlar?' he asked. Astonished, I replied that I was. 'I'm a Fetlar man,' he enlightened me without preamble, 'My name's Jim and I'd like to say – welcome!' Jim was Dorothy's husband.

Being a dyed-in-the-wool 'soothmoother', I was full of apprehension as to how the local people were going to feel about me – about such a strange-looking person, wearing a religious habit, landing in their midst. So Jim's welcome had both touched and encouraged me, and as it turned out was to be the beginning of a friendship with his wife, which would influence the whole of my life. Dorothy, hailing from Edinburgh, was a professionally gifted woman in the world of drama, and a superb teacher. She later became the adjudicator of the Shetland Drama Festival.

The next morning after this incident, and on arriving in Lerwick, Jim persuaded Rosemary and me to travel with him to Fetlar in his car rather than squashing into the furniture van we were accompanying. It was at this juncture in SOLI's history that Rosemary had determinedly travelled north with me to 'settle you in', as she had said. Subsequently, of course, she too was to move from Devon to join me on Fetlar, though at that time and to put it in her words, she thought 'the whole venture to such an end-of-the-world sort of place, total madness'. Of course, I had wanted her to fall instantly in love with Shetland, but just like the thing, it was one of those grey, extremely murky April days, and the only comment I remember her rather dolefully making to Jim, as we drove along, was that she would not be surprised to see 'a Viking boat loom out of the gloom'!

Once on Fetlar, Jim dropped us at our destination and, driving away, called out that we must visit his home soon. 'That is as soon as you're properly settled in. My wife Dorothy will want to meet you,' he yelled.

In due course Rosemary had returned to her home in Devon, and since I was not connected to the telephone in those days, Dorothy kindly invited me to visit her and Jim each week for a cup of tea, her idea being that Rosemary could ring me there. So it was that over the months, which turned as they do into years, Dorothy and I discovered that we had a lot of things in common, and as already said, not least cats! Hence a lasting friendship developed.

Every so often, before she and Jim eventually moved to live on Yell, Dorothy would visit me at The Ness, and once in a while we walked down to the beach below the house. On one occasion I remember our spending the whole afternoon leaning up against a boulder, with the tide creeping nearer, and talking poetry. That was when I learned that among her many creative gifts she also was a writer. It was soon after this that my publishers wrote asking if I would consider writing my story, or, they said, would you like someone to write it for you? Rosemary, who was staying on Fetlar at the time, announced in a trice that she would be willing, and that I could illustrate the book. 'No,' I had heard myself determinedly, and with some surprise at my own audacity, answering, 'I'm doing it myself.' Whether I was able to write was another matter, but this was where Dorothy came in. A week later, when telling her of the incident, I found that her enthusiasm matched mine. 'Well,' she demanded, 'have you started yet?'

'Yes,' I replied, nervously. 'Would you be interested to see my efforts?'

Passing her four sheets of paper, I refrained from saying how long and hard I had laboured over them, or that, in the end, I had felt quite chuffed with the results!

Ten slow minutes later, Dorothy pulled her chair into a more comfortable position and looked up. 'Now, you're probably aware that you shouldn't share your writing with anybody, certainly while it's in its infant stages. Folk reading it could easily give you the kind of negative criticism that would cause you to shelve a really good idea before it's had a chance to germinate in your own mind. However, I think that under the circumstances, you can feel safe with me . . .'

'Is it awful, then?' I asked.

'No,' she murmured, after an ominously long pause. 'There are a few promising ideas . . . however, I'm afraid that the first page needs scrapping!' Looking directly at me, she continued, 'You might be able to use part of it, elsewhere of course. But really, it's much too passive.' She pulled another page across the table. 'Now, what I suggest is that you try using one of your later paragraphs; this one, for instance.' She pointed to the appropriate sentence. 'This bit about the "grotesque little gnome-like men . . ." Yes, start the book with that. It's a punchline which will make your readers wonder what on earth you're leading into. And that, of course, is the whole point, for they'll want to read more!'

So in this way I was instructed, and even now, several books later, I still use the rather tired sheet of notes which Dorothy originally typed, listing the most important things a writer needs to remember.

Yes, she was a woman who added enormous richness to many lives, and not least to my own. With regard to religion we had numerous discussions, most of which ended with our agreeing to differ. However, there was one conversation which stuck in my mind more than the others, and it was connected with a Fetlar sunset. The experience was deeply spiritual, and one I felt she would always carry. Touched by the element of trust which prompted her to share it with me, I now – and especially since her death, which just happened to fall on my birthday – remembered the radiance the experience gave her. As I wrote my tribute, I thought of that awaiting glory which she herself had now entered, that wonder far surpassing any of this world's sunsets, even in Shetland! Unexpectedly, Halliaria Kirk popped into my mind, where at a certain time of the year the sunset slipped behind the crest of the hill, was eclipsed for a second or two and then emerged on the other side in a flare of sunrise. The glory at the so-called end of our life was the same, I supposed, and the hill was death; we moved from one side to another in just a fleeting eclipse . . .

Early on the morning of the funeral I set off over the Mainland from St Mahri's Hame to the ferry terminal and drove on to the boat. Boat trips were surprisingly pleasant, for one could pause from, probably, miles of driving and sit comfortably in the car and read, snooze, knit (not that I am given to knitting) or whatever else. On this occasion I read through my tribute, which by then had turned into a mini-sermon.

Almost an hour later, having driven the 18 miles up to the north of Yell, I crunched to a halt outside the kirk. A little early for the service, I found an open door and, creeping inside, sat in the silence of the church, praying and continuing to consider my friend's life and death. Before long, the church began to fill, and a moment or two before the minister arrived Rose slid into the seat beside me, giving me a warm feeling of home! Rose was on Yell that day in her professional capacity as a nurse, for she sailed over from Fetlar for a few days each month to do a part-time nursing job. Having discovered that much renovating work needed to be done in Lower Ness, she had taken the employment partly to help her put the house to rights. On return to Fetlar from the south of England, Rose had spent almost a year attached to SOLI as a Seeker, discerning whether God was calling her towards the vocation of being a Sister or a Companion.

After the service, we followed the long procession of cars to the burial ground ten minutes away from the kirk. Then, standing around the open grave, with the wind gusting sand across the dunes and biting into our faces, we looked over the waters to Fetlar. Although the view was bleary and the day bitter, Rose and I both had the same thought of what a wonderful burial place it was. A stone's throw away, the sea simmered, and as we stood, our heads bowed, the on-going life of my friend became strangely discernible. A sudden lightness came into my heart – an uplifting! Raising my head I watched the coffin being lowered into the grave. The human body, that earthly temple of the spirit, had been vacated, and with every bit of honour due to it, it was laid in the earth to which it belonged. Indeed, it may sound a strange parallel to make, but as her body was buried, her spirit it seemed, rose to the fulfilment of a new and glorious chapter. Someone sobbed in front of me and others dabbed their eyes, and sorrow seemed, just for a moment, a strange thing.

Undeniably, saying goodbye to people we loved was painful, for bereavement was often a wrenching apart. Nevertheless, many of us during a lifetime received that odd glimpse of the 'beyond'. If only more people, I thought, could apprehend that our loved one's departure was only the beginning of a new bonding, and perceive, if only blearily, what lay behind even so thin a veil. Perhaps, I pondered, this earthly part of our journey could be likened to a babe in the womb. The womb was a dark place, yet it was also somewhere comparatively safe, a place where we were still being formed and where we were not yet ready to understand or be lifted into the fuller picture. Probably, here in the womb of the world we were also maturing, growing like embryos towards a fuller understanding, wholeness and perfection; towards that day when we would burst forth into the reality of the immortality to come . . . And with what expectancy those eternal ones on the other side must wait for our emergence!

My feeling of elation remained. Christ's disciples must have felt much the same when he left them at the Ascension. They knew that they would no longer see his form in this world or be so conscious of his presence, yet there was the knowledge of a new fullness of being and it was something indescribably uplifting. That day on Yell was an experience of a similar nature, that of a soul being lifted into the wholeness of Love.

Later, I drove across the island to the ferry terminal still thinking of Dorothy, sensing her presence, even finding myself having a little conversation with her in my head, and in fun suggesting that she could always answer me with a rainbow! It may have been a coincidence, but if it was it was certainly one that startled me out of my wits, for a rainbow suddenly appeared, and spreading its arc above, spanned the sky!

Once over the ferry crossing, I covered the miles back across the Mainland, driving into the setting sun. Wilma had insisted that I called in for a bite of supper, and after the meal I rumbled up the slope to St Mahri's Hame where, wasting no time, I said Compline and went to bed.

A day or two passed, with only a telephone call from Sister Mary Aidan to say that she was having a lovely time in Norfolk. Work went well and I felt happy that I had come. However, that blissful state was not to last, for another cloud was soon to scud across the skies of life, causing sorrow to grip the heart.

Taking a second or two to untangle the appallingly jarring noise from a dream, I eventually translated the sound in my mind to that of a telephone. Leaping out of bed I flew along the passage, and, not a little shell-shocked, picked up the receiver. It was Sybil.

'Mother, I'm sorry to ring you so early but Mooskit isn't any better,' she sighed. She had rung the evening before, so I already knew that he was not eating and was sleeping a lot. 'He's been lying on that green cushion in your room, but I've now carried him downstairs. Don't worry too much: he's very peaceful, but not wanting to get up or to eat, and he's not meowing or purring.' Since Moosy was always a vocal creature and one that never missed a meal, this was worrying. Over the past few months he had been diagnosed with a thyroid problem, which Sybil and I had been treating with daily doses of pills. Rather wonderfully the medication was working well for him, and in an earlier phone call Sybil had told me that he was healthier than we had seen him for months. 'In fact,' she had said, 'he's just brushed past me and looks absolutely blooming . . .'

Literally days later, I could tell from the tone in Sybil's voice that there was something horribly wrong. The previous evening I had urged her not to worry, just to give him a little more time. We felt it more than likely he had eaten something which had disagreed with him. Now, shivering in the hallway, knowing that if I were to dash home I would need to catch the earliest ferry (a 45-minute drive away) there was not a moment to lose. I said to her, 'I'll come . . . See you in a few hours.'

Having carried Mooskit down to her sitting room the night before, Sybil had made him comfortable and kept vigil. Shuna, unexpectedly appearing from her dog bed upstairs, had slid into one of Sybil's best armchairs and curled up. Together in the firelit room with the moon shining over the sea, they had kept Moosy company. Sybil told me later that it was a special and somehow holy night, though how she wished that Moosy was doing all his naughty little things, those antics which had so exasperated her and were in the same tradition as Skerry and Flugga before him.

For her, she told me, it had been a night of asking God to heal him and grant us a few more years, or at the very least a few more months. Likewise, I also prayed as I sped across land and sea back to Fetlar. After Flugga had died, Mooskit had moved into the privileged position of being the only cat, which suited him well, for somehow, despite being such a strong character, he had for most of his life been the slightly aloof number three. It was not that God did not want to answer our prayers with some miracle, but simply that we did not always ask for the best thing. How he stretched our faith in this way, I thought, testing our responses and making us strong, through pain and disappointment.

When I arrived home, Mooskit was lying on the comfy bed Sybil had made for him on the floor, and as I walked into the room and saw him, I heard myself announcing, 'He's dying.'

'Yes, I think so,' Sybil gently reiterated, 'though he's very peaceful. Do you think we could just allow him to die?' I was in a quandary, for I knew that I must return to St Mahri's Hame that same afternoon. Sitting with the little fellow for an hour, I could see that his condition was not going to change speedily, and so decided that we could only act upon the advice of the vet. As it turned out, the vet's over-the-phone prognosis for Mooskit was not hopeful, to which he added that cats could sometimes take days to die; therefore, he thought the best thing would be to bring him over to the Shetland Mainland that night. Deciding to catch the next ferry, we transferred Mooskit's bed on to the seat beside me in the car and, leaving a heartbroken Sybil at the doorway, I set off.

Our car goes by the peculiar name of Tobias, due to its registration letters equalling 'Raphael On the Passenger Seat'. A bit twee, but never mind; I knew that it was always good to have an angel companion with us. Anyway, I would not have been at all surprised if St Raphael, the archangel of all the healing angels, might not have been holding our darling Mooskit as I drove into the darkness to the vet's that night, and indeed helping me as I squinted sideways so many times to check his breathing.

The vet, who had stayed on at the surgery to await our arrival, took us immediately into a consulting room. My strong grey friend, one of the biggest cats we had ever known, suddenly looked very old and worn, and having rapidly dehydrated was by then unable to stand on his legs without being supported. However, true to character, there appeared nothing weak about his spirit as he clenched his teeth to prevent Colin from looking into his mouth. 'His temperature's sky high, and that probably points to an infection, in which case there could be some hope . . . Look, let's try to get his temperature down overnight, and I'll see him again in the morning,' Colin had said, brightening up. I could not believe my delight. The young man gave me a syringe with which to get water down Moosy's throat, and since Sybil had managed to get him to lick ice cream off one of her fingers, Colin recommended that I try something similar, to give him energy. After an antibiotic and cortisone injection, I popped him back into the car and we sped on to Mahri's Hame. An hour later, and full of renewed hope, I settled him on my bed, and not long afterwards joined him. On the stroke of every hour, the little puss licked custard off my finger and took a few globules of water. To my amazement, by 2.00 a.m. he was actually sucking a whole syringe of liquid and even managing to lick custard from a saucer held under his chin. After that I snoozed intermittently, though found to my amazement that he called me with a barely audible squeak on the dot of every second hour. My memory now was of our once fiercely independent and princely Mooskit trusting himself totally to my care, struggling to hold up a pink nose, opening his mouth to the syringe, and allowing me to wipe his running eyes with cotton wool. I was sure he understood . . . There was something incredibly appealing about him, and, as it had been for Sybil, special about the night. By the morning, which was actually the feast of St Raphael, I awoke and stretching out a hand stroked him. Unbelievably, he purred! I was beside myself, for he looked so much better. Ringing Sister Mary Cuthbert and Sybil at once with the good news, I told them excitedly, 'Mooskit's going to live!'

The vet was delighted that Moosy's temperature was down to normal and suggested I left him at the surgery for a couple of hours, so that he could take some blood. Later, and full of thanksgiving, I returned to collect him. Ushered into the consulting room I knew instantly that something was amiss. Holding out a small phial filled with yellow liquid, the young man wasted no time in telling me, 'This is all I can get from him. You see . . . he's very jaundiced . . . And . . . actually, his liver and kidneys have completely packed up!'

'So, you mean there's only one answer . . . ?' I whispered, tears already pricking my eyes.

A nurse brought Mooskit into the room, and on the feast of the great archangel of healing, we gave him back to God. Interestingly, only a second or so after the needle was injected into his leg he died, and the vet nodded that he must have been on the very brink of going.

Shocked, and with a heavy heart, I took the body of my little companion back to Mahri's Hame and carried it in its box up the narrow stairway to the loft chapel. There it was to lie for a couple of days until, finally, I returned to Fetlar. In an extraordinary and totally unexpected way, I felt the pain of his passing physically. But this was only a cat, you must be thinking. Yet long ago I knew a man who buried a dog whom he had dearly loved. Buying a small tombstone, he had had it inscribed, and placed it on the grave. If I remember rightly, it read, 'And you, too, shall have a little golden crown!' Yes, every creature created by God was about loving, and naturally pain was all part of the package.

Sister had left a basket of ironing and, glad to have a practical job on hand, I pulled out the ironing board. As I moved the iron back and forth, thoughts came to me again, of our Lord's Ascension, and, as at Dorothy's funeral, the heaviness of saying farewell was strangely lifted. In fact, I felt as though my own hold on life was suddenly loosened. But then, that could be so for any of us . . . for if we were open to the truth of Love, it would always bring freedom. Did the disciples at our Lord's Ascension experience this same release and spark of glory? They were certainly elated, for, as the scriptures had told us, 'they had returned to Jerusalem full of joy, and spent all their time in the temple praising God'.

That first night after Mooskit's death I of course missed his presence, particularly when I went to bed. The syringe and the saucer of custard were still on the bedside table, and the hot-water bottle that I had tucked in beside him was still waiting to be emptied. There must have been all sorts of reminders to the disciples of Christ's beloved presence, too . . .

Lying down, I closed my eyes, asking God only for 'peace'; and in spirit holding the little cat in my arms, I slept.

12

The Spirit of Love

Excitingly, Rose's reception as a Novice Companion was upon
us. The ceremony had been arranged for the feast of St Raphael,
though because of my absence we had transferred the festival
until the day after I arrived home from St Mahri's Hame.

It was late when the car rolled to a stop. Sister Mary Cuthbert
greeted me, opened the passenger door and carried the box
containing Mooskit's body into the chapel. Placed on a tiny table
in front of the altar and covered with a white cloth (as we had for
Flugga), it was to rest there overnight and throughout the Sung
Eucharist the next day. Rose had said that she did not mind in the
least sharing her service with a little grey cat!

So the next morning the candles were lit, and with the chapel
aglow, the organ voluntary began to weave its melody into a
crescendo of sound, until it faded to a whisper as I entered with
the words of the Welcome and then, walking to my stall, said the
opening sentences of the Mass.

Our Lord Jesus Christ said:

'. . . You shall love the Lord your God
   with all your heart, with all your soul,
   with all your mind and with all your strength.'

The second is this:

'Love your neighbour as yourself.'

There is no other commandment greater than these.[1]

With this great admonition, we were led into the worship of God, and the service took its course. After the Gospel, Rose left her stall to kneel before the altar. We too, with that lovely sense of anticipation, familiar with such occasions, knelt in our places, while Jean, sliding on to the organ bench played the introduction to the hymn:

O Thou who camest from above,
    The pure celestial fire to impart
Kindle a flame of sacred love
    On the mean altar of my heart.

There, let it for your glory burn
    With inextinguishable blaze,
And trembling to its source return
    In humble prayer, and fervent praise.

Jesus, confirm my heart's desire
    To work, and speak and think for thee;
Still let me guard the holy fire,
    And still stir up thy gift in me.

Ready for all thy perfect will,
    My acts of faith and love repeat,
Till death thy endless mercies seal,
    And make my sacrifice complete.[2]

During the last verse I moved forward to receive Rose's public declaration of an already abiding commitment to God, and to make her a Novice Companion of SOLI. From different parts of our chapel, we, her spiritual family, circled around, our voices resounding, singly or in unison:

In the name of the Father,
In the name of the Son,
In the name of the Spirit,
 Three in One.

If we take the wings of the morning
and settle at the furthest limits of the sea,
even there your hand shall lead us
and your right hand shall hold us fast.[3]

With that lovely ebb and flow, and in a great intermingling of joy with the odd trace of sorrow, for Mooskit's little box was still present, the service moved on:

One thing have I desired of the Lord;
one thing I seek.

That I may dwell in the house of the Lord
all the days of my life.

To behold the fair beauty of the Lord
and to seek him in his temple . . .[4]

There were many calls and many different kinds of vocation, though for SOLI, both as individuals and corporately, there lay at the heart of them all the reality of God. For us, his presence was paramount, and he, Love Supreme, was most powerfully shown forth through those two great commandments of Love with which we had opened our service. First, his love was centred within the temple of our human hearts, the temple of our humanity . . . and second, at the hub of our oneness with each other – our unity as a community in this place. Such a bonding of love, culminating at that moment in our small wooden chapel, also extended to all those whom our lives touched, both near and far. Thus, Love our God was ever present within the temple of both our individual and corporate soul, and whatever our vocation, it spun from this axis of love. Stemming from such a source, we could be sure that no calling, however exalted or humble, was any greater than another, for the greatest vocation for any of us was that to which we, personally, had been called. Our only real concern was that we should be faithful. Recently, a visitor, staying for a longer period than most was asked, 'How is the community treating you?' Her reply was, 'I feel surrounded by love'! It seemed to me, that if her response was the only thing SOLI ever achieved, then our work would have been worthwhile.

Like the early Carthusian lay brothers, who cared for the hermit monks in a number of practical ways, shielding those whose job was to keep the contemplative fires burning at the centre of their religious life, our SOLI Companions were similar, though somehow grown in wholeness. Starting with our Founding Companion, Rosemary, the vocation of SOLI Companions both protected and radiated that Christ-centre which lay at the heart of the life. Their call, which might be described as a less restricted way than that of the Sisters, allowed for a larger degree of independence, for with its different obligations the Companions, if they wished, were free to embrace a more active role in a sense of service, and certainty of relating on a day-to-day level with those outside our hermitage-cells. Nevertheless, in the sense of prayer, Companions shared the contemplative aspects and focus of the life. So, generally speaking, they were those who had been called to the living out of the Mixed Life – a mixture of both the contemplative and active parts of a spirituality, as opposed to the more defined hermit vocation. They did not make vows, but instead made promises, and they had an honorary life membership of SOLI, though they could make an actual commitment for life if called to do so. Those who did were known as Companion Donates, or in other words Companions who had donated their lives to God. So, although they did not make vows as such or were bound by the same rules as the hermit, it was a calling akin, for it stemmed, from the same origin, from the same vocation of love. Whatever the differences between the Sisters and Companions, both lived within a framework of life, and in loving loyalty to the Mother and Chapter of SOLI.

Rose had thought long and hard about her calling, and at this stage still had future options. Again there was that spiralling element attached to our life . . . that flexibility of movement, and that essential maturity of being able to revolve into an appropriate sphere.

The service gave me especial joy, since we were delighted that Rose had returned to Shetland. I looked up, for we had reached the solemn ceremonial part, with the Novice Guardian's words of:

Mother, we present to you Rose, a Seeker of SOLI.

Turning to her, I asked, 'Rose, what do you request?' and she replied:

In the presence of you, Mother,
and you, my Sisters and Companions,
and you, my friends,
I request to be received as a Novice Companion
of the Society of Our Lady of the Isles,
and to the best of my ability and with God's help,

to live out my commitment
in the loving fellowship of this family
for as long as the Lord shall ask.

Accepting her request I placed my hands on her head, saying:

Rose, we accept your request
to become a Novice Companion of SOLI,
and pray that the Lord our God
will bless you in your calling.

So Rose began her walk along the path which would more than likely lead her towards becoming a full SOLI Companion. She was choosing at that moment, as Sybil and Jean had chosen before her, to dovetail her life into that of the Sisters, and to participate in their daily life at a deep level. She had a life-plan of her own, which she would follow joyfully, and renew her commitment to annually.

A Companion, then, was one who lived in her own home, alongside the Sisters in vows, and who supported herself financially. She was one who acted as a strengthening element to the life, helping protect the spirituality at the heart of the community, which meant shielding the Sisters, when possible, from too many of the outer pressures. The Companions were the inner 'circle around', as opposed to the Caim, being the outer 'circle around'. Yet as well as leaning inwards towards the Professed Sisters, they were also watchful in the outward direction, often acting as a bridge or a stepping stone to Caim Members, visitors, friends, searchers, islanders and strangers. This being so, they needed to be persons of great discretion. The Companions made it easier for the Sisters to fulfil their particular lifestyle of building up a power-house of prayer, a place of perpetual communion with God.

With my hands still on her head, Rose made her commitment, saying:

> Almighty God and Father,
> I, Rose, give to you
> all that you give to me,
> all that I am and will be.
>
> Therefore,
> in the presence of this my spiritual family
> and these my friends,
> I promise to walk in your love,
> to live in your service
> and to lovingly fulfil my calling
> as a Novice Companion
> of the Society of Our Lady of the Isles.

I stepped back and Sybil, as a fellow Companion, came forward to say the following prayer:

> God be with you,
> in this his day,
> every day,
> and every way,
> with you and for you,
> in this his day.

With Rose now thoroughly welcomed to a deeper level of commitment, Jean then took up the refrain, with a psalm of praise. And after all our prayers I turned and blessed the Companion's brown, cowled tabard, folded on the altar. Rose would wear this religious garment in chapel and on any other appropriate occasion, with of course the SOLI cross she had originally been given as a Caim Member, a simple wooden Celtic cross, worn by us all who belonged to SOLI.

Lifting the robe, with these words:

> Rose, we give you this tabard
> as a garment of salvation
> and symbol of the yoke of Christ

I placed the tabard in Rose's hands and, placing the cross around her neck, said the following prayer:

> Carry Christ's yoke with joy,
> and around your neck his cross,
> the sign of God's eternal love.[5]

Rose, drawn by the God of love, had been accepted as a Novice Companion and at a later date, if she were willing, her commitment to 'Love alone' would be ratified and made absolute.

Clothed in the tabard, Rose continued to kneel at the prayer desk, while fresh strains from the organ carried us into the singing of 'St Patrick's Breastplate':

> Christ be with me, Christ within me,
> Christ behind me, Christ before me,
> Christ beside me, Christ to win me,
> Christ to comfort and restore me.

> Christ beneath me, Christ above me,
> Christ in quiet, Christ in danger,
> Christ in hearts of all that love me,
> Christ in mouth of friend and stranger.[6]

The hymn ended, and again I placed my hands on Rose's head in the final blessing:

Rose, may your sleeping be blessed
with contentment and untroubled.
May your waking, and your work,
and all that you do, however lowly,
be holy, a life-prayer to the glory of God.
And may you serve God for ever,
for the love of the Father who created you,
the Son who redeemed you
and the Holy Spirit who strengthens and guides you.
Rose, Novice Companion of SOLI,
may the Lord bless you now and always.
Amen.

As Christians, we all of us needed to recommit ourselves daily, and within the Eucharist was the perfect place. It was a place of gathering together, as the Apostles had gathered at Pentecost. For them, the Holy Spirit had descended in tongues of fire. At our Mass that day, in celebration of St Raphael, we had reached the point known by the Church as the 'Peace', and where we, of SOLI, made our peace before renewing the offering of our lives to God. Afterwards we would move forward into that fiery place of participation, into the Eucharistic Prayer, into the Consecration . . . into the receiving of the Holy Dove!

As always, and if possible even more so with every Mass, the words of Consecration lifted me into another dimension. With hands outstretched over the bread and the wine I knew that I was a channel, reaching through the veil of time into the eternal. Warmth tingled my fingers, and there was a growing sense of other hands taking mine. Were those spiritual counterparts of ours – Our Lady, the Apostles, our beloved ones who had passed through the invisible veil, those whom our earthly eyes could no longer discern – closer than we could guess? Was heaven, at that moment, taking hold of earth and lifting it into the communion of Love, lifting it into Christ, the Christ now consecrated in the holy bread and wine of his body and blood? 'If I be lifted up I will draw all men to myself,' he had once said. And he had been lifted up – on the cross, at his Resurrection, at his Ascension, and now was lifted high in this glorious Host, drawing us all into himself. At this awesome moment and at the elevation of the holy Host of Christ, there was the utter silence of union with God, and also of our union with each other. 'I in them,' Christ had said, 'and you in me, that they may be perfectly one.'

At last the service concluded, leaving us with those hints of glory I knew and loved so well. We had been touched by something extraordinary: by love, by Love our God, by Love his Son, and by the infiltrating power of the Holy Spirit of Love who bound us in one . . . and who bound all our joys and sorrows into glory.

Back in the sacristy, I exchanged the white vestments which I had worn at Mass for a red stole, and returned to chapel. Our business was not yet finished. Pulling forward the tiny table, we stood around it.

The words were not easy and I paused, intending the prayers to be short on that day of festival and rejoicing. We thanked God for the enormous love that the gift of Mooskit's life had given us . . . for all those personal and precious memories of such a unique friend. But most of all, in our hearts we gave thanks for the traits of trust and loyalty found in every creature who knew it was loved. Our Creator had given us those dear ones for our comfort and pleasure and, I was sure for our learning, and also that we might know and receive that extra ounce – that extra lick – of love! Indeed, he had given Mooskit to us, and now he had taken him home to himself. We could not deprive God of that, by any selfish clinging. Silently, I prayed to him to help me to allow Moosy, and all those who had died, animal or human, to be free . . . and also to assist all who mourned, in whatever way, especially those tossed between the knowledge of eternal truth and their own emotional feelings of separation and pain. May they find that same peace, as I, I inwardly murmured, and may they and we grow through pain, positively, to a new crowning of love in heaven.

I lifted the box from the table . . .

> O loving Christ, may they rest in peace, and ever share your risen life in glory. Amen. Let us go forth in peace, and in the joy of the Lord . . .

We processed up to the rockery garden where Skerry and Flugga were buried, and there Sister Mary Cuthbert sprinkled soil over the small container as it was placed in its grave. Finally, using the same words as we had used for Flugga,

> 'Ashes to ashes, dust to dust.'
> Death into life, and life into God . . .[7]

we said the final prayer together:

> Cry out with joy to the Lord, all the earth and its creatures, worship with gladness and enter the Lord's presence in the fullness of life. Amen.[8]

13

Love Glorified

Another New Year was imminent and all too soon the old would be gone. Short though the day had been, it had gifted us with a measure of blue sky and sunshine, and half an hour before Vespers I took Shuna outside to the garden. There, I stepped over the lowest bay of rockery fencing and walked up the sloping bit of field beyond. In Fetlar, the bumpy piece of grazing was called Craa's Knowe, or in English, Crow's Hillock. Actually, it always reminded me of the Hill of the Angels on Iona, and I wished that I knew the Shetland word for angels! In the early years of living at

Sister Mary Cuthbert, Kelpie and hens

The Ness, I had sometimes walked Rosemary's little dog there. Suddenly I heard echoes reverberating down through the years of 'Come along, Tikki, though only around the knob today.'

That afternoon, standing on the bump of land and feeling not unlike St Columba (if only!) I glanced around at my beloved community. Jean was striding down the road from her tiny hermitage home of Bethany, towards Lark's Hame, carrying a basket of washing. Rose was getting out of her car outside Lower Ness; and at The Ness itself Sister Mary Cuthbert, fast becoming an expert gardener, had disappeared into the croft house from the bare-looking vegetable patch and chicken runs. She must have been checking that the hens had put themselves to bed. Apart from tidying up, fertilizing the ground, mending the fences or a few other jobs when possible, gardening did not much employ us during the winter, and even in the warmer seasons in Shetland it was always something of a risk because of the wind. All the same, this year it had paid off; and now we were looking forward to a 'Shetland-proof' poly-tunnel being erected at the back of The Ness in the spring. We could hardly believe that the tunnel, which would make the germination and early growth of our crops so much more reliable, had been gifted to us. Darkness began to drop, and the barn, attached to one side of The Ness, looked stark. We had at last succumbed to having its felt roof removed, though were still waiting for a builder to come over to Fetlar to replace it more substantially. Larger skylights were to be put in along the south side, and Sister hoped that she would be able to use the building in a multipurpose way, maybe as a greenhouse, definitely as a store and, who knew, perhaps part of it as a place in which to grow mushrooms.

The absence of cats around our dwellings of SOLI, especially down at Lark's Hame, seemed sad, though none of us would be at all surprised if, in the not too distant future, a 'peerie kettlin', as they sometimes called them in Shetland, sallied forth!

Swinging around, I saw a light flash on in one of the windows of Tigh Sith, our visitor accommodation, and guessed that Sybil had carried over a batch of new cards or other items she had for sale. Seeing movement, I reckoned she was setting them out in what we ambitiously called 'the shop'. A moment or two later the light went off and she emerged from the building and walked towards chapel. The Chapel of Christ the Encompasser, as always, both warmed my heart and pleased my eye, for it stood proud and beautiful, especially on a winter's day as it fell into dusk.

Wondering what Sister Mary Aidan would be doing, I decided that I must ring her after Vespers. Normally she was here with us over the festive season of Christmas, New Year and Epiphany, though on this occasion she had for several reasons felt it necessary to stay on the west side. She was sad not to be here, of course, and we too were missing her a lot and determined that such a thing should not happen again.

Peering around for Shuna, I called her, and at the same time glanced across the bleak landscape along the coast, just discerning the silhouette of another hill upon which stood Weatherhead, the property where Frances had lived. At the moment, Jane, who had visited us during the summer, was using the house for six months in order to have time to think about her future. Later, we would welcome Janet, arriving to begin a process of discernment with the idea of testing her vocation to SOLI. These arrangements of 'time out' for both women had taken grit, for Shetland could be a hostile environment at this time of the year. We often heard people from the south, mostly summer visitors, remarking that although the isles were lovely for holidays, they could not possibly live in such a bare, treeless place, especially in the wintertime. Effectively, however, there were many advantages to having no trees, for one could see the shapes of the rounded hills, the uncluttered sky and seascapes, and those often misted and perpetually changing horizons. In point of fact, we had been told that long ago there must have been many trees on these islands. Trying to conjure up how Fetlar might have looked with pine trees thrusting spiky heads into the clouds, I found myself suddenly transported to a piece of woodland in the far reaches of my own past in Devon, to a place called the Drumbles, a place which I had known and loved, and from where I had dreamed of the future. What my eyes surveyed now, actually living in that future, bore only faint resemblance to my dream, and none to that lush Devonshire spot. No, there were no trees here, though in an awesome, metaphorical sort of way, I supposed that in effect we ourselves were trees!

Shuna came to heel and we made our way back to Lark's Hame. Leaving her in the house I went into chapel, where apart from a flickering lamp I sat in the gloaming. Memories of Rosemary and her little dog had brought to mind how we had a few times walked up to the Drumbles together and sat under a certain tree . . . We had known the piece of woodland well, and had used it separately, as a 'thinking place', as a place set apart.

The Drumbles was a landmark to the locals who lived around it – in the cottages, working in the fields or travelling, mostly by tractor, along the deep-set country lanes. However, although people were sparse in that area they did very much include the inhabitants of a small thatched-roofed convent, which nestled into the skirts of the hill. The Sisters, as you might have guessed, were the Franciscans to whom I, and briefly Rosemary, belonged, and where we helped tend their 36 acres of field, garden and woodland.

Despite the knoll being such a feature of life to all who came and went in those parts, few ever took much notice of it, or could be bothered to trudge to its brow. In fact, to most it had become of little use and, as already said, only a landmark. Nevertheless, there were a few people who were aware that in at least one era of its past it had rejoiced in a significant measure of glory, for tales were told, generally by older folk, of its prestige as a Roman fort. Of course, by the time I was introduced to it all signs of that period had long since disintegrated into the loam. Indeed, only the swaying branches retained any mystery of its past, in their whisperings and in the stretching of their arms heavenwards. So it was that as time went by, I too became enamoured of this small grove of trees, in a constant longing for my next visit, for I found it the perfect place to escape all the strictness of a tightly packed schedule. Hence, I climbed there whenever the community's weekly two hours, known as 'recreation afternoon', permitted, for it was a place where one could be sufficiently detached from a lifestyle, so as to be able to view it from both a deeper and yet greater height.

Sitting in our far northerly chapel, I appreciated those days now as being an experience of retreating into a dimension of the heart, for in touching the heart of the wood, in a strange way one touched the heart of God, and in doing that, glimpsed a corner of the soul and, had I known it then, SOLI.

So those lucid summers were of many a snatched-at hour, of sitting under the shade of a particular tree and week by week delighting in the rotation of rural life. There was a cornfield that sloped away from where I sat, and beyond it a vista of pine trees, which always produced in me a strange nostalgia for the north. And there, at the edge of the wood, perched on gnarled roots I would dream, stare or write poetry.

Alas, all too soon, as you will appreciate, time flashed by, for it took half an hour to walk up to the Drumbles and the same amount of time back, back to the feeding of pigs and hens and to the round of being a Sister, as well as to all the work and prayer and prayer and work which that life involved. In this way the seasons came and went, yet for me the little wood was always there, silently waiting, and more and more it became a place set apart, a hermitage, a place to be with God.

Somehow, whether it was a remote island knowe, an ancient site on the top of a Fetlar hill, a copse of trees on a Devonshire hilltop, this, our little chapel, or the temple of the soul, they were all focal points and God-centres of holiness.

Yes, I thought, we, in ourselves and as a family in God, were not unlike the Drumbles, for we were a place set apart. It was the same too, I supposed, for every Christian, although for some their being set apart was more pronounced than for others. Even so, we were all a living part of God's greater design, part of a forest of forms, habitats and colours. And although all of the same species (for trees were trees and humans were humans), individually we were each different, ranging from the wildly flamboyant to the quiet, hidden woodland sprigs. This being so, to my mind it seemed that we should not try to emulate each other too much, but rather, concentrate on being who we were, within the landscape in which we had been set. God, our Master Gardener, planted his saplings of many shapes and shades, and each grew to size at a differing rate and was unique. Of course, it was that variation of kinds which created the overall changing shape of the wood, a shape which could be seen to advantage by our occasionally stepping back, and seeing ourselves as the Gardener or as others saw us, for in this world we were external as well as internal people; each special, with all the joys and difficulties which went with our nature. In other words, continuing to use the metaphor of woodland, this was why our leaves were so varied and why some trees were tall and others short, some hardy and others more prone to this or that disease. This being so, for the contemplatives to step back now and then to consider the outer, exterior side to life was imperative, otherwise they could fall into the old adage of not being able to see the wood for the trees. It was also equally necessary for the active souls of the world to step into the heart of the wood for a while, and there to experience new depths of 'being'.

As we had so often found, it was the same when looking at SOLI: everything was always a bit clearer after one had stepped back to see the picture in its greater entirety, and from a selection of angles. Of course, it was better still if at the same time we were able to incorporate our knowledge of the interior details of the life; all those little things which pressed so closely around us, the overgrowth and the ivy, and a whole thicket of things which impeded, as well as all the other lovely ones too, the sprouting forth of new growth, and the bursting into flower of new insights which gave joy.

So, in an incredible way, and indeed in more ways than one, it seemed that there were parallels, and that we, SOLI, individually or as the family in God, set in our bare Shetland landscape, could be likened to the Drumbles, to a woodland which stood on a hill and had become a landmark to many. Of course, it was precisely because of our altitude and because of our being viewed so easily that we would often find ourselves judged. Galling though that could be, it was perhaps no bad thing in the end, since as witnesses of the God who had called us and planted us for a particular purpose, it was absolutely right that we should be sized up, and very natural, that, with the world being as sceptical as it was, our characteristics should be evaluated. Whether the world was qualified to assess us correctly was a different matter, and one, I guessed, which was of small account.

So SOLI, like a clump of trees on a hill, would continue to be looked upon and criticized by some, barely noticed by others to whom it had probably become altogether too familiar, and possibly written off as being a bit useless or not worth approaching by many more. Nevertheless, thank God, there would be others who, seeing it from a distance, would hopefully see a beautiful merging of colour and shape and would be drawn nearer, and in their drawing near would find, perhaps with surprise, that it was not so much a group of curious individuals of interesting types which was the attraction that drew them, but instead, and so much more importantly, the aura of a quiet, sacred place, within which could be grasped the mystery and peace of Christ. They would find that what had really attracted them was the emanation of God himself, and that what they had seen in SOLI from a distance was simply the outer encirclement of God's own abiding: a human tabernacle of the Almighty, a tent formed by God of like-minded souls, grouped together by their Creator for his own purpose and praise, though principally for the accommodating of his glory! SOLI was like a wooded glade in which stood Christ. Around him grew the oak, elm, ash, a beech and a pine, a silver birch, and maybe even a prickly holly or two, all standing together as a holy temple of God, imperfect, yet with an intermingling of boughs reaching upwards.

The chapel lights flared on, illuminating the walls and the fine lines of the building. Two figures came in, genuflected and silently knelt in their stalls. I too knelt, and gradually the community began to arrive for Vespers and Mass. Thoughts of such a collection of different people reminded me of an incident which had happened a few years before, on the day I was made a deacon in St Andrew's Cathedral, Aberdeen. A small group of us were having supper with the bishop and his wife, and the conversation revolved around the Enneagram system of describing human personality types. To my shame, I as much as said that I thought the whole idea a bit silly. Gracious, I would not have believed that such argument could have ensued! Everyone, including Sister Mary Clare, Sister Mary Aidan and Rosemary, all rounded on me. At first I was embarrassed, then determinedly unbending . . . so much so, that indignant traces of the experience remained until comparatively recently when I was given a little book by Sister Mary Aidan. It was called *The Enneagram*, and much as I dislike saying so, I found it fascinating enough to read several times over, and certainly appreciated that we had been talking at cross-purposes on that ill-recalled evening. Indeed, I came to believe that there were, in all probability, a definite number of personality types, and even more amusingly, that God just might have sent one of each of them to SOLI!

So, to sum up, we as people were undoubtedly of one species known as human beings, in the same way that the Drumbles was of one species known as trees, but both were made up of various types. Placed together, those types could be interesting, strong and even beautiful. They could be looked upon from afar or in close proximity. They could stand together strongly, because, in all probability, they had been planted together for the living out of a purpose. Inevitably, people would ask, 'But of what use is a place like the Drumbles?' or 'Of what use is SOLI?' Others would be indifferent or antagonistic. However, many would find that within the shade of both there was shelter, refreshment and joy; a refreshment not of any earthly making but of God, for it was God the Almighty, himself, who dwelt at the heart.

Finally, I felt sure that in every instance, God did not create such temple-like places as the Drumbles to be utilized only as the world thought fit: that was, in the sense of temporal objectives; though timber had a great many more good, rather than exploitive uses, such as the building of hospitals, schools, factories and homes, the manufacture and publication of God's word on paper, or a multitude of other essential purposes. It was similar with people, I decided. Active religious communities, social services, devout lay people, politicians and others provided for many of the obvious needs of the world – healing, education and so on – all the acclaimed ways in which both the trees of the woodland and people, and in particular, in this context, religious communities, could be used for the service and care of humankind. However, there was just one tiny, hardly considered thing to be added to the list, a usage rarely rated high, either with regard to trees or people, and that was exactly what Rosemary and I had found at the Drumbles, found in the little woodland that had outgrown any obviously important use. It had simply given us itself; it had just stood, seemingly doing nothing – and how far-reaching had that been?

Yes, there was something sacred about the wood, with its tree-tops interlaced as though into the traceries of some great paradisal church. It was a place where one could lie and listen to God's music, to wood pigeons cooing, to a woodpecker tapping, or to a whole symphony of other winged creatures contributing their praise. There was the light, too, filtering through the leaves, dappling the paths and catching the undergrowth, bringing everything to life in a new and amazingly sharper and more glorious way. The sunlight illuminated swathes of bluebells, transforming their hues into the indigo and aqua of heaven. It was certainly a place indwelt by God.

The Drumbles

I saw now that for Rosemary and me, the Drumbles' not so very obvious reason for being was exactly like SOLI's, for by its very nature its purpose was a hidden one. Many of God's children had been asked to live hidden lives; indeed, Christ's own life was almost entirely so, as was his mother's. Without doubt, God did not only work through his so-called 'active' disciples, but equally through the secret, sometimes silent ones, who, I have to stress, were in fact truly active, only in a different way! Mary of Nazareth, later to be assumed and glorified in heaven as queen of all the saints, and who unceasingly reaches out to us now to draw us to her Son, was one such person . . . Mary, hardly mentioned in the Gospels, was, within the mysteries of God, the most humble of all souls to be made great and glorified.

So, like the Drumbles, SOLI stood – simply being itself. In a multitude of ways it was imperfect, blemished and carried deep scars, yet it continued to stand strong for all those who had eyes to see and hearts to perceive. Some of its branches were broken, it had certainly seen better days, and in the natural course of things, a tree or two had died. There were other gaps, too, for other reasons, due perhaps to the ravages of storm. But still the woodland of SOLI had its own beauty – the beauty which was of the Almighty, himself – a beauty, which was the Almighty – and a deep, silent purpose, which was his will. To many, to the travellers, seekers, strollers, dreamers, the needy, the weary, work-worn people, who entered its shade, it would be a refreshment of soul, a place where they could be still and silent, and where, immersed and centred in God, they could catch glimpses through its leaves of heaven, or from its periphery catch other, more earthly aspects or horizons of their own lives in this world.

Everyone was now poised for Vespers to begin, and silently I charged my spiritual family to abide in Love:

Through Love our God, I charge you, the Society of Our Lady of the Isles, to rejoice . . . to rejoice in simply being yourself . . . in standing high in the witness of his glory . . . in standing strongly together and at one, in the bond of your calling, despite any of the gales, buffetings or injuries of the world. I charge you to rejoice in the providing of a place of abiding for Christ, a sacred place of worship and praise, of refreshment, joy and peace . . . a conduct for his glory. And may he, our same Lord, bless you and give you joy everlasting . . . May he make his face to shine upon and through you – that you might touch the hearts of his children with the light of his love; and may that same love be your own crowning in heaven. Amen.

Epilogue

Life for most of us is made up of those things which we perceive as real, a series of eventualities woven with sorrow, joy and a few hints of glory, which seem to some just a random route, beginning with birth and ending in death. Yet I have come to think that this limited perception of our existence tells us little of the real truth.

Incomprehensible though it may sound, I feel that we are continuously poised on the brink of wonder! We are physical yet also spiritual beings set in a universe of many dimensions: a place of movement and merging, ebb and flow, and where, emanating from Light, we are spun into a cycle of light, into a spiritual galaxy where God is our Centre and our Sun. As Christians, of course, we are moulded by God into a shape patterned on the life of his Son, Jesus. So, to my mind, our life is like the symbol I have used of a spiral, a vital force, where within its convolutions we pass through experiences which are often familiar, and are drawn into situations and to places where we get an inkling that we have been before and will, maybe, visit again at a different level, height or depth, and where we constantly touch Christ. Meanwhile, in that contradictory way of the world, we live in the gravity of the present moment, in the 'now' of this instant, in a state which I believe will end when that final circuit of earthly life swings us into the beginning of what will be, into that greater fullness of

God. We cannot know the time or the hour of that moment but can only move forward towards it in hope . . .

Having recited the dawn-hour Office of Prime, I gaze over a cold winter's sea and, beyond it, to layers of new beginnings. There, I am carried into the remembrance of one – of a long ago winter where this story began . . .

Springing up in bed, my only thought was to glance outside for reassurance. Yes, joy, fresh snow drifted across the window, and behind the patterned swirls of ice made by Jack Frost, the white wonderland was still there. Flakes sliding an inch or two across the pane briefly compacted before fusing into a whole patchwork of other shapes. My heart bounded, and in a thrice I threw back the bedclothes and pressed my nose to the glass. Then, hurling myself down the stairs, I cried 'Mam, can I go out and slide? You tode me I cud this mornin.'

'I want ta goo an mek a snowman,' said a sleepy voice from the top of the stairs.

'Not before yav both had ya breakfast. Ya need some food down ya, first. Now go an get washed and dressed, then we'll see.'

Back in my bedroom, with my mouth close to the window-pane, I puffed out a warm stream of breath, making a peep-hole through the ice, then dressed, hardly able to take my eyes from the snowy glimpses of that 'other world'.

There was no dawdling that morning and soon we were sitting around the breakfast table, with a coal fire crackling in the hearth. 'Now don't gulp, there's plenty of time. Yav got all day,' said Mam, 'and ya Dad's goin out with ya, ta shuvel paths before next lot cums down.'

At that moment Dad came in, and knocking a bowl of ash from his pipe on the grate, pulled up a chair and asked us if we would be going into the garden to help.

'Dad, ya not shuvelin it all off a paths, are ya, cos it'd spoil it?'

'I want a snowman Dad,' Carole chimed in.

It was Saturday, so there was no school, only the anticipation of a whole day of undiluted bliss. An hour later, togged in warm clothes and itching to get out, I opened the back door. My younger sister, four and a half years younger than me, was still sitting on one of the kitchen stools, with Mam waving a gumboot at her. 'Stick ya foot out, me duck, let's get this last wellie on.'

Standing on the doorstep I gazed, awestruck, though suddenly hesitant. It was all so smooth, so perfect, and yet inviting. The trouble was, if I trampled into it, the scene would be changed, churned up and spoiled. If only I could fly or could embrace the snow without destroying its loveliness. The urge to slide, however, was far too great a desire to resist for more than a moment, and I stepped gingerly out, my leg sinking deep. Drawing in a breath of wonder, I took another step forward, and another. Then, turning, I called back to my squealing sister on the brink of launching herself out of the door. 'Yuv gotta walk in my footsteps, Carole.'

'No, I want to go this way . . .'

Carole bumbled around, knocking wodges of whiteness from the bushes. Dad followed, pulling her from the drifts and showing her how to roll huge balls of snow for the snowman. Wading to the top of the garden I found a piece of path where the wind had blown the snow thinner; hard and glistening, it was ideal for a slide. Starting to make it at once, I slithered across its icy surface with all the fearlessness of youth. Soon it was a proper slide and over and over I ran towards it, speeding down its glassy course. One had to risk abandoning oneself, yet a certain balance was also needed, and only then came that faint indication . . . that flash of 'freedom and flying' . . .

Rising from the stool in the pointed window of Lark's Hame, another day with its own unforeseeable twists beckons us forward, beckons SOLI forward, beckons a new sliver of the world forward into its light. Through the earth's dark history there have been many new days, which have drawn men and women into the light of Love. Trails of people have taken their routes – scientists, musicians, artists, poets, billions of ordinary and extraordinary souls, seekers of the truth. Sometimes the path has been slippery and treacherous and, falling, they have needed to rise and start again. Often caution was needed, though sometimes they have dared to abandon themselves into the exhilaration of their quest. Today is another such new and joyful beginning, for us and particularly for our friend Janet, since we are making her a Seeker. With SOLI, she will now move forward into God, and, hopefully, like us will do so solely for God, for Love, alone . . . . SOLI DEO.

Notes

Chapter 1 Love's Call

1 Genesis 1.3, Revised English Bible.
2 Hymn which is used in SOLI Small Hours is taken from *The Divine Office* (Society of St Margaret, East Grinstead, published by Oxford University Press, 1953).
3 Prayer adapted from *Celtic Vision*, by Esther de Waal. (Dartman, Longman and Todd).

Chapter 2 Love Conceived

1 John 12.24, REB.

Chapter 5 Love Presented

1 'Nyook' is a Shetland word meaning 'nook'.

Chapter 7 Love's Sorrows

1 2 Corinthians 6.10, NRSV.

Chapter 10 Love Resurrected

1 Isaiah 61.11, REB.

Chapter 12　The Spirit of Love

1 Scottish Liturgy 1982 (published by the General Synod of the Scottish Episcopal Church).

2 *The New English Hymnal* (Canterbury Press, 1998).

3 Psalm 139.9–10, NRSV, adapted.

4 Psalm 27.4, AV, adapted.

5 Prayer, adapted by +MA from *Hebridean Altars* by Alastair Maclean (The Moray Press).

6 'St Patrick's Breastplate', from *The New English Hymnal*.

7 'Ashes to ashes, dust to dust', from The Book of Common Prayer (Oxford University Press).

8 Based on verse 1 of Psalm 100.